NOT
FADE
AWAY

THE ONLINE WORLD REMEMBERS JERRY GARCIA

N O T
F A D E
A W A Y

THE ONLINE WORLD REMEMBERS JERRY GARCIA

Edited and with an Introduction by:
DAVID GANS

Foreword by:
STEVE SILBERMAN

Picture research and photo editing by:
f-stop **FITZGERALD**

Photographs by:

RICHARD McCAFFREY

BARON WOLMAN

JIM MARSHALL

PHILIP ANDELMAN

JOHN ROTTET

MALCOLM LUBLINER

f-stop **FITZGERALD**

THUNDER'S
MOUTH
PRESS

A BALLIETT & FITZGERALD BOOK

Photographs:

Front Cover © f-stop Fitzgerald 1995
Back Cover © Richard McCaffrey 1995

pgs. 14, 16, 18, 19, 21, 23, 26, 29, 30, 32, 35, 36, 38, 40,
43, 44, 48, 50, 55, 61, 62, 66, 71, 72, 76, 77, 79, 84, 87,
88, 94, 95, 96, 102, 103, 105, 108, 110, 111, 112, 114,
118, 120, 122, 124, 126 © Richard McCaffrey 1995
pgs. 10, 13 © Baron Wolman 1995
pgs. 82, 85 © Jim Marshall 1995
pgs. 17, 75, 80, 90, 101, 106 © Philip Andelman 1995
pgs. 49, 56, 65, 68, 93 © John Rottet 1995
pgs. 24, 28, 52, 58, 67, 74, 117 © Malcolm Lubliner 1995
pgs. 3, 60, 98 © f-stop Fitzgerald 1995
poster pgs 46, 60 courtesy Bill Graham Archives
Lyrics by Robert Hunter, used by kind permission of Ice Nine Publishing Company, Inc.

Book design: Béatrice Schafroth

Not fade away: the online world remembers Jerry Garcia/edited and with an introduction by David Gans; foreword by Steve Silberman; photographs by Richard McCaffrey… [et al]
p.   cm.
Collection of messages posted to the Internet by Grateful Dead fans upon the news of Garcia's death on Aug. 9, 1995.
ISBN 1-56025-125-5
1. Garcia, Jerry, 1942-1995. 2. Rock musicians—United States—Biography. 3. Grateful Dead (Musical group) 4. Internet (Computer network) I. Gans, David.
ML419.G36N68   1996   95-44952
782.42166'092—dc20   CIP
[B]   MN

First Printing 1995

Printed in the U.S.A

Published by

Thunder's Mouth Press
632 Broadway, 7th Floor
New York, NY 10012

Distributed by

Publishers Group West
4065 Hollis Street
Emeryville, CA 94608
(800) 788-3123

A Balliett & Fitzgerald Book

Balliett & Fitzgerald Inc.
Executive editor: Tom Dyja
Photo editor: f-stop Fitzgerald
Cover design: Sue Canavan
Assistant editor: Maria Fernandez
Research: Howard Slatkin

Individuals interested in original photographs from this book should write to:

f-stop Fitzgerald,
c/o Balliett & Fitzgerald Inc.,
66 West Broadway, Suite 602, New York, NY, 10007.

for reet   **— dg**

to Boomer, long may he rock   — fsf

A C K N O W L E D G E M E N T

This book happened in a hurry. I wanted to assemble a text that spoke in many voices, and I am thankful to all the WELLheads and netheads who offered their thoughts without prompting and responded positively when I asked for permission to include them in this book. Not a single person said no when I asked.

My wife, Rita Hurault, gave up a lot in the month between Jerry's death and the completion of this manuscript; I am grateful to her for her patience and support in this instance and for more blessings than I could ever enumerate.

Steve Silberman gave generously of his words and spirit, and at the very last minute dropped by to make sure the text was just exactly perfect. Likewise Blair Jackson, friend and neighbor and colleague, who performed some last-minute script doctoring.

Thanks also to my agent, Sandy Choron, for keeping an eye on the long view as well as the short deadline; Goldie Rush, for keeping it together in the name of Truth and Fun; Carolyn Garcia, for sage advice, as always; Phil Lesh, Gary Lambert, and Dan Levy, friends and colleagues and fellow trustees of the Eyes of Chaos Foundation; Regan McMahon; Dennis McNally, with whom I have had a profound and mutually educational relationship for fifteen years and counting; Keith Karraker, who made his words and his time available just when they were needed most; Elaine Zablocki and Diane Driver, who poked around in all the right places and shared the results; and Deb Trist, who passed along some magical text.   **— dg**

Thanks to all the photographers — Jim Marshall, Baron Wolman, John Rottet, Philip Andelman, Malcolm Lubliner, and especially Richard McCaffrey; to the Bill Graham Archives for gracious use of posters from their collection; to Ice Nine Publishing for allowing use of lyrics; many thanks to Joan and Chris at Atlantic Photo and special thanks to Jack Reale, freaky Frank, and skinny Mitch Cohn for dragging me to Alfred, New York for my first taste of the Dead and finally to our publisher Neil Ortenberg.   **— fsf**

TABLE OF CONTENTS

A ROSE IN CYBERSPACE

by Steve Silberman

Good grief.

That's how Wavy Gravy, quoting Charlie Brown, characterized the rippling outward of intense feeling through the fabric of humanity that followed the news of the death of Jerry Garcia.

There were vigils in Strawberry Fields and Golden Gate Park, an homage from President Clinton, drum circles and singing circles, and frank and passionate tributes in newspapers all over the earth. Fellow musicians like Bob Dylan, David Crosby, and Mike Gordon of Phish told the world how Jerry's music, humility, and respect for the living tradition had inspired them. At Haight and Ashbury, an altar sprouted from the cracked pavement, heaped with roses, photographs, poems, and drawings; incense was lit in the shrine room of the largest Buddha in North America to hasten an auspicious rebirth of Jerry's spirit; and over one bricked-up door of the old Fillmore East (scheduled for demolition that week), a Deadhead posted a portrait of the guitarist at work, under Michelangelo's hands of God and Adam, reaching to touch.

Jerry had spoken a universal language of the heart in his music, and the universe answered with an outpouring of generosity at his death.

Deadheads did what they do best: they came together. For many, it was the resources of the online community that enabled them to reach out, to feel fellowship rather than isolation in their great sadness, and to mingle their tears and praise with those of kindred spirits.

Since the days when the Internet was young, and Paul Martin of the Stanford Artificial Intelligence Lab compiled a mailing list for ticket information, Deadheads have helped make the Net a human place. They wrote software and stashed coy lyric references in the code, developed and populated networks and bulletin boards, and enlivened chat rooms with spirited schmoozing about the tapes, the touring, and the epiphanies that seemed to arrive more readily at Dead shows than elsewhere.

I was logged into the WELL when news of Jerry's death arrived in a burst of onscreen messages—including one from David Gans that read simply, "Can this be true?"

In the following days, as the world learned more about the depth of Jerry's accomplishments as a musician, Deadheads learned about the extent and the creativity of the Deadhead community.

Within hours of the announcement, scores of virtual candles had been lit in the halls of cyberspace. Lovingly-illuminated Web pages went up, as interlinked as Deadheads themselves have always been, inviting readers to add their own stories. Chat rooms on America Online filled with Heads sharing information, memories, and song lyrics, which now spoke to them with deeper poignancy. On the WELL's intimate and scholarly Dead forum, memorials were organized, journalists were guided to informed sources, and the oceanic flux of emotions was given a focused vehicle of expression.

The online world gave Deadheads a rallying place to make things happen in the offline world: to make a cry to heaven, and then plant seeds of healing on earth.

If there's one story in this collection of practical miracles that resonates most deeply for me, it's the tale of a single rose.

As head of Grateful Dead Ticket Sales, Steve Marcus knows Deadheads' hearts, being the recipient of thousands of fancifully decorated envelopes and letters over the years from Heads seeking tickets to the shows. As a member of the WELL, Steve was also one of the first members of the Dead's organization to become an active participant in the online community.

During Jerry's funeral at St. Stephen's Episcopal Church, Steve understood how much his friends online would have wanted to say goodbye to the man whose music (bearing the wise counsel of Robert Hunter's lyrics) taught them to rely on one another. The stories in this book—and many others that will be told until the end of our days— are the petals of the rose that Steve placed in Jerry's hand, in the name of online Deadheads everywhere.

A gift from the garden to the garden.

Steve Silberman is coauthor of **Skeleton Key: A Dictionary for Deadheads**

I'LL SHOW YOU SNOW AND RAIN

by David Gans

As the guitarist and vocalist and leading songwriter of the Grateful Dead, America's best-loved rock band, Jerry Garcia had the straightest line from the heart to his fingers of any musician I have ever heard. His playing was all about expression. This book is about the expressions of shock and sorrow and spirit and worry and mourning and compassion and celebration and wonder that attended his death.

Garcia was fifty-three years old when he died—ancient by the sad standard set by Jimi Hendrix and Janis Joplin and the Dead's first frontman, Pigpen, and others; too young by decades by more reasonable measures of human life. A brilliant and eloquent composer and improviser, Jerry and his guitar made hundreds of thousands of people extremely happy for a very long time, providing along the way, in word and deed, a stellar example of right livelihood.

Over the course of their thirty-year career, the Grateful Dead have performed live for more people than any other band in history. Theirs is a great American success story. They prospered by delivering a quality product to a satisfied crowd, and by doing it reliably over a long period of time. Garcia's death by heart attack on August 9, 1995, brought one of human history's most profoundly pleasant trips to a sudden halt.

GOLDEN GATE PARK, 1976
RICHARD McCAFFREY

The magic of the Dead's music—a real-time experience rich in subtleties that takes some effort to comprehend and rewards repeated contact—is hard to translate to the uninitiated and irresistible to its adherents. The narrative quality of the Dead's art encouraged the formation of community, and the strength of the bonds among the members of our community is the real subject of this book. Most of the people who loved Jerry Garcia never met him, but they felt intimate with him just the same.

There is nothing simplistic or bombastic about the music of the Grateful Dead, and Jerry's playing covered a broad emotional terrain. In his (and the Dead's) heyday, the musicians were as interactive as you can be—now out in front with a solo, now intertwining with another instrument in melodic pas de deux, then overhauling the entire rhythmic underpinning with a sequence of perfectly placed chordal stabs. As garrulous as he could be with his axe when the occasion required it, Garcia was one of the best listeners ever to buck the stereotype of the "lead guitar."

To those who feel that connection with the music—and the character—of Jerry Garcia, his death is much more than the loss of a favorite entertainer; it is a true

WARFIELD THEATER, SAN FRANCISCO, 1980
RICHARD MCCAFFREY

life-crisis, more so than most cultural transitions, and more so than practically any political milestone. It is no exaggeration to say that in the world of the Grateful Dead, life as we know it has come to an end, and an immense social and economic network has been thrown into chaos.

The first phone call I got on August 9, 1995, came at 8:30 A.M. from my sister in Arkansas, who read a one-line item on the news wire and wondered if it could really be true that Jerry Garcia was dead. Dire rumors had come around many times in the last ten years, but they didn't usually show up on the news. I did what just about everybody else does when such a call comes in: I turned on CNN. Within a few minutes the bad news was confirmed. The details were pretty sketchy, but the fact was inescapable.

The phone began to ring nonstop, as word spread among the huge and highly communicative global family of Deadheads, and the media began its pursuit of comments and information from visible Deadheads such as myself, Blair Jackson (author of *Goin' Down the Road* and *The Music Never Stopped* and publisher of the great Deadhead fanzine *The Golden Road*), John Dwork (editor of the other great Deadhead zine,

Dupree's Diamond News), and Steve Silberman (coauthor of *Skeleton Key*: A *Dictionary for Deadheads*). All the television networks, NPR, local radio stations, newspapers, and magazines were on the story instantly. The Grateful Dead have been good copy for years, and the band had been in the news recently because of a near-biblical series of catastrophes that had plagued their tour just a month ago.

It began to sink in that the unspeakable had happened.

At around eleven o'clock on the morning of Jerry's death, I drove to the Berkeley studios of KPFA to appear on NPR's "Talk of the Nation" with Blair Jackson and Steve Silberman, followed by an interview with Pacifica Network News; I then charged off to downtown Oakland to make a thirty-second appearance via satellite on a Seattle TV news show. After that I returned home to await two camera crews from ABC and CNN, and I discovered that my new answering machine was pitifully inadequate to the demands of a day like this one. I returned as many calls as I could, from friends and family and reporters all over the country.

I live in an odd zone between the "inside" and the "outside" of the Grateful Dead world. I produce and distribute a weekly radio series, the "Grateful Dead Hour," a travelogue of the wide musical world of the Dead. I've also written two books on the subject. I am seen as an insider by most people, because I am closer to the band than most. I am most definitely an outsider at times like this, though, because I am a fan and an associate and a friend and a licensee, not an employee or a family member. At a time like this I face away from the band and speak to and for the public. It seems to be my role in this movie to present the best of their music to the fans and to help non-fans understand why this man was so important to so many people.

KPFA is my radio home in the Bay Area; I do a two-hour show every Wednesday night. I brought in some records and a few favorite tapes, and went on the air at seven with the sweetest passage of Grateful Dead music I know: the jam from the first-ever "Wharf Rat" back into "Dark Star," recorded February 18, 1971.

WARFIELD THEATER, SAN FRANCISCO, 1980
RICHARD McCAFFREY

"There's no easy way to break this news to you, but Jerry Garcia was found dead this morning," I began. "The entire world is on this story, so I don't imagine that you're hearing it for the first time from me now, but it is true. The unthinkable and the inevitable has happened. Jerry's gone." Gary Lambert, editor of the *Grateful Dead Almanac*, joined me in the studio, and we opened the phones. We learned that vigils were taking place at hundreds of locations around the country; no one wanted to be alone with this dreadful news. We heard great stories, notices of other gatherings, outpourings of grief and gratitude—everything you would expect members of a close-knit subculture to express at such a monumental moment.

After the end of the two-hour broadcast, I came home and logged into the WELL, my online home and the hub of a tremendous amount of Deadhead communication. Earlier in the day, I had been unable to read anything due to the tremendous number of people reading and attempting to post messages online; when I got through at ten o'clock, I saw more than a dozen new topics representing the thoughts and feelings of hundreds of people who were torn up by the news.

TRIBUTE TO BILL GRAHAM, MARIN CIVIC CENTER, SEPTEMBER 29, 1984
RICHARD McCAFFREY

My wife and I were booked into the romantic hillside Casa Madrona hotel in Sausalito for a romantic weekend starting Friday, August 11—a wedding gift from Phil Lesh and his wife. Having been told there was no public memorial, and having postponed Casa Madrona earlier in the year due to a family emergency, Rita and I decided to go ahead with the weekend getaway.

As we were leaving our house in Oakland, I got a call alerting me to a wake at the Fillmore Auditorium in San Francisco. This was for all the Grateful Dead and Bill Graham Presents employees and other outer family who weren't among the 250 or so invited to the funeral. Four o'clock until whenever, we were told. So we drove over to Sausalito, crossing paths with mourners fresh from Garcia's funeral which took place Friday afternoon a mile or two from the Sausalito waterfront, where we were headed. Less than an hour after checking into Casa Madrona, we were up to our ears in traffic on the Golden Gate Bridge, heading into San Francisco to join our friends in mourning.

US FESTIVAL, 1982
RICHARD McCAFFREY

My wife said it reminded her of backstage at a Dead show; the Dead tapes playing on the sound system made it feel—just a little—as though you might walk around the corner and find the band on stage. Every single person of the hundred or so who were already there was someone I saw at one or another of virtually every Grateful Dead concert in California.

The people in this room had relationships with the Grateful Dead that ranged from imaginary to fiduciary, and had relationships with me that go back more than twenty years.

"All these people whose names I don't know are as familiar to me as my own family," I confided to a woman whose name I didn't know, whom I'd seen hundreds of times at shows.

"You probably don't know my name," she said slyly. If the Dead scene had been a small suburban town, she would have been the woman who lived two blocks away, whom I waved to as I drove past in my station wagon. She told me her name and smiled.

I had brought my tape recorder with me to the Fillmore, and I went around the floor asking people to "tell me a story." I heard from women who had gone to the movies with Jerry; a cab driver who scammed his way backstage by claiming to be the taxi that Rock Med had called for; tape collectors who finally have enough time to properly annotate their collections.

The mood of the gathering was summed up by one woman who told her hilarious story of meeting Garcia at a college radio station way back when and concluded by stating, "I just don't know how I'm going to get through life without ever seeing that man play the guitar again."

It wasn't until August 13, when 20,000 deliriously grieving human beings gathered at the Polo Field in Golden Gate Park to dance and cry and say goodbye, that I finally made the time to begin acquainting myself with my own thoughts and feelings about the passing of Jerry Garcia, to whom I owe more moments of pleasure and insight and truth and fun than I could ever count on nine-and-a-half fingers of forty thousand hands.

The Dead and the city of San Francisco and Bill Graham Presents made the memorial service happen on very short notice. If they had given us a week to gather for it, the city would have been overrun, and the true purpose of the gathering would have been drowned in distractions. Ultra Sound brought the Grateful Dead's sound system for the occasion, and BGP painted a huge portrait of a grinning Garcia to watch over the

festivities. On the benches below the portrait, an altar was laid out with candles and pictures and flowers, and over the course of the warm afternoon people lined up to make offerings of unimaginable material and spiritual dimensions. My wife Rita was one of the people who performed the service of receiving these gifts from the celebrants on the field and placing them among the treasures at Jerry's feet; this is a partial list of the things she carried: flowers, beads, crystals, joints, rings, shoes, socks, hats, t-shirts, photos, cookies, candles, incense, balloons, buds, earrings, poems, prose, sobriety tokens, pinwheels, prayer flags, drawings, rocks, guitar picks, guitars, zucchinis, troll dolls, a tiny Barbie, bread in the shape of a lightning bolt, rose petals, Buddhas, Gumbys, saints, madonnas, and wrapped-up satchels containing who knows what. Of all the wonderful, sacred, and silly things people placed on that altar, my favorite by far was a donut—a "foot" donut, like the ones they sell at the Dream Fluff donut shop in Berkeley—with one of the toes missing.

BOB WEIR AT HOME, 1979
RICHARD McCAFFREY

It was a day filled with reunions and partings, of flowers dropping from the sky and white doves flying into it. Friends who never met, but knew each other from decades of shared pleasure in what we all know to be the safest place on earth, stopped to introduce themselves at long last— not to say good-bye but to acknowledge that we will be together again, and soon.

Vault archivist Dick Latvala asked me to help him with the music for that memorial, and we knew we had to make those speakers sing with the best. Dick brought suitcases full of DATs and cassettes, while I prepared a handful of the sweetest and most appropriate passages I could gather. We did what the Grateful Dead do: we improvised, and let the moment tell us what was required. When we learned that the band members were going to speak, it was Dick's inspiration to follow with "It's All Too Much" (a song from the Beatles' Yellow Submarine soundtrack that Vince Welnick brought into the Dead's repertoire in 1995) and the longest, happiest "Iko Iko" in recent memory. After that I played that sweet jam from February 18, 1971. We had a sacred obligation, and we took it to heart. And when you're talking Dick Latvala, you are talking serious heart.

It all came to a head for me during "The Wheel" and "Box of Rain," played at top

volume. Looking out at all those familiar faces, wondering when we'll be able to gather again in joy rather than sorrow, remembering the amazing adventures . . .

A few years ago a guy started showing up at Dead shows wearing a bear suit that lit up. All night long, he'd dance up one aisle and down the next, spinning an LED-festooned scepter as his bear suit flashed. One night I introduced myself. His name was Rob Levitsky. At the Polo Field memorial, Levitsky danced tirelessly all afternoon beside the altar—in his bear suit with the lights turned off—waving a pair of long wands with brightly-colored ribbons streaming in the breeze. I watched him for a while, confronting the possibility that I'd never again follow him around the Coliseum from the corner of my eye, never again say hello as he passed my seat on his delirious trajectory.

Each one of us has hundreds of these casual brethren to account for in our hearts, by way of preparing for the rest of our lives. This sort of thing must happen to everyone who grieves over anything: at random times, the thought strikes me as never before that The Good Times Are Over. They aren't, of course, but they are. Some peaks will never be scaled again. I'm about to turn forty-two, entering my prime, but I'm also getting eyeglasses for the first time, and I have to begin serious consideration of my next career. My life has changed in ways I cannot yet contemplate. The phrase that comes to mind over and over again is, ironically, the title of a recent Phil Lesh composition: "Childhood's End."

For the Deadhead community, the death of Jerry Garcia means the end of many pleasures. For the musicians, I can't figure out if it's the end or a beginning. This story-teller makes no choice—that's up to the players. As I write this, exactly a month after Jerry's passing, the band's musical future is a question mark visible in the sky from Fennario to Deer Creek. By the time this book is in the reader's hands, we'll probably know whether the band is continuing. But today, everything is up in the air. Think of this book as a hand-canceled postcard from that moment.

The concern we felt for Jerry in his last difficult years is now afoot in the world as free-floating compassion. Jerry's death brought many processes to a screeching halt, called many issues to immediate resolution, brought many grievances to spontaneous forgiveness. I saw miraculous reconciliations in those first few days; I was the donor and the recipient of a few of those myself. It is a wonder and a blessing.

Sorrow and pearls, my friends. Our box of rain runneth over.

This book literally would not have been possible ten tears ago, because the online world as we know it today did not exist. But when Jerry Garcia died, Deadheads all over the planet shared their feelings across the vast electronic reaches in an online gathering that went on 24 hours a day for several weeks. Hundreds of thousands of heartfelt messages were posted.

Not Fade Away is a collection of some of the most eloquent and affecting material from that online wake.

The moment the news broke, the Grateful Dead conferences in the WELL (the general gd conference; the deadlit conference, where we talk about literary and musicological matters; gdtapes, where the recordists talk technique and swap their wares; gdtours, the site of road-trip planning and concert reports; gdtix; and gdh, the "Grateful Dead Hour" conference) were overwhelmed with responses from grieving Deadheads. Much of the material posted in those areas is intimate, articulate, impassioned, and somewhat inaccessible to the uninitiated reader because of the richness of our common vocabulary. Discussions appeared in several non-Dead-oriented confer-

WARFIELD THEATER, SAN FRANCISCO, 1980
RICHARD McCAFFREY

ences, including news, genx, and politics; it was in those places that Deadheads explained their hearts in plain English to a general audience and that's also where some non-Deadheads discussed their own surprisingly deep feelings about the passing of Jerry Garcia, whose exploits they did not follow closely but whose life, they suddenly discovered, made a difference in our times.

Average citizens and famous personages speak in exactly the same type size on the net, identified only by name and e-mail address. This book presents personal stories from Deadheads and non-Deadheads from many walks of life: a Connecticut psychologist, a Berkeley chemistry student, a Los Angeles schoolteacher, a San Francisco attorney, an Alabama oral surgeon. Stewart Brand, founder of *The Whole Earth Review* and a participant in the Acid Tests with the Dead and Ken Kesey (both represented in this book), created the WELL as an experiment in 1985 and watched the Deadhead community charge in and create a thriving online culture. Carolyn Garcia, "Mountain Girl" of Prankster fame and the mother of Jerry's daughters Annabelle and Teresa, graciously allowed me to include a transcript of her remarks at a memorial in Eugene, Oregon (which had been posted to the net immediately after the event). David Grisman, who had known Garcia since they were young bluegrass fans chasing Bill Monroe around the country with a tape recorder (and who recently came online with "Dawgnets"), sent an eloquent tribute. Peter Grant, who played pedal steel guitar on *Aoxomoxoa*, tells about the day he and Garcia got the idea to take up that instrument. Wavy Gravy offered a haiku that he wrote on the day of Jerry's death.

The Dead have always had articulate supporters in the rock press. Richard Gehr offered the tribute he wrote for the *Village Voice*, while Al Giordano of the *Boston Phoenix* and Mikal Gilmore of *Rolling Stone* contributed more intimate pieces to the net than they were able to write for traditional publication. Steve Silberman and Gary Lambert — long-time Deadheads who, like me, have found ways to make a living in the Deadhead culture — have also offered stories and impressions.

What all of these people have in common is an appreciation of the extraordinary life and music of Jerry Garcia, who made hundreds of thousands of people extremely happy for many years. There aren't enough words in the language nor pages in the book to encompass the pleasure and meaning that Jerry delivered in his lifetime; this book is an attempt to gather a variety of perspectives in hopes of transducing a little of the magic.

— *David Gans*

CHAPTER I

MIRROR SHATTERS

GREEK THEATER, BERKELEY, JUNE 14, 1985
RICHARD McCAFFREY

JEFF GORLECHEN

It would be like if tomorrow you heard that there is no more baseball. No one can play or watch it—it is no more. You can watch old tapes of games and read accounts in old newspapers, and everyone would know what baseball is but no one could experience it again. No more little kids playing Little League. Nothing. That's sort of what happened here.

PATRICIA MORRIS

Wednesday morning, around eleven, I was in Chicago, driving down Lakeshore Drive, enjoying a brief respite from the intense heat and humidity with the car windows

POTRERO HILL, SAN FRANCISCO, 1968
MALCOLM LUBLINER

rolled down. I was reveling in the morning and one of my favorite drives in the country, the lake to my left, the skyline on my right. That bold skyline that, for me, carries the energy of both profane power and sacred mysticism. I had WXRT on the radio, loud, when they made the announcement. "We have very sad news from the music world this morning . . ." The voice was as heavy as the ten-ton truck barreling down the far lane next to me. It was the one thing I most did not want to hear.

I burst into tears. They played the announcement by the Marin County Sheriff's Department. XRT had waited to go public with the news until they had absolute confirmation, because of the many rumors of the past. They played snippets of interviews with Jerry and, of course, they played the music. I had been thinking about extending my stay—too many people to see and not enough time. But suddenly, I wanted to go home at once.

I drove on, tears rolling down my face, digging in my purse for Kleenex, trying to keep it together to remember where I was and where I was going. I arrived at an Italian restaurant called Rico's where I was meeting a friend, a sixty-year-old Oak Park lawyer,

SPARTAN STADIUM, APRIL 1979
RICHARD McCAFFREY

for lunch, my eyes swollen and red. While I waited for him, the TV in the corner of the bar made the announcement. The wait staff gasped. They stood stock still, and their eyes filled with tears.

So did mine, again, and my lip quivered as I told my friend when he arrived how upset I was and why. He wasn't into the Dead at all, but he got it at once, and was kindly sympathetic.

After lunch, I had to drive three hours west to where my family lives. Driving across the prairie, covered now with verdant fields of corn and soybeans and thick stands of hardwood trees. Everything there seems so solid, so substantial, so earthy, but that's not how I felt. Every hour XRT did an update and played a set of Dead tunes. Every hour I drove on and sobbed. Thunderstorms rolled in. The sky became black and rain poured down.

I stopped at the home of a cousin to mourn. He and his family were at the last show, one month ago that very day, at Soldier Field. We reminisced, we told stories, we sat in silence.

Driving on that night, a magnificent light show lit the prairie sky. Bolts of lightning flashed and crackled across the southern horizon, from east to west, bouncing between billowing clouds, connecting heaven and earth. There was no doubt in my mind, heart, soul, that this was no ordinary thunderstorm. This was nothing less than Jerry's guitar licks emanating from the heavens.

CHUCK CHARLTON

"Wall Street Week," in the opening monologue, mentioned only two significant events of the past week: The IPO of Netscape, and the death of Jerry Garcia.

AL GIORDANO

Move aside, Elvis. Roll over, Beethoven. I saw Jerry last night.

Like Tom Joad in Steinbeck's *The Grapes of Wrath*, Jerry will be seen every time people break through the boundaries of the limited "reality" our species has agreed upon. "What did the life of Jerry Garcia mean?" asked Chris Lydon yesterday morning on Boston public radio. I answered, "Freedom."

Anyway, last night I decided to treat myself to a special dinner at a French restaurant alone. I sat there smoking my tobacco, and a young waiter came up to me: "Are you bummed about Jerry Garcia?"

SPARTAN STADIUM, APRIL 1979
RICHARD McCAFFREY

"Yeah, man. Very."

"My dad called me today in tears," said the waiter. "It was only the second time I ever heard him cry." He told me what it was like to be a child raised on Garcia. Said he plays the banjo and the French horn in a ska band. Said he was going to Africa with the Peace Corps in September. "I'm so glad you're here," he said, "nobody here understands."

Jerry lives in that twenty-one-year-old young man.

ALAN CHAMBERLAIN

I was talking with a colleague this morning about some stuff, and he says "So, I heard Jerry Garcia died this morning. What does that mean?"

I told him, "For one thing, it means there aren't going to be any more Dead shows." And then it hit me. Up until then I was feeling pretty okay about it—I mean, he had a very full life, left behind a huge body of work, etc., so I wasn't feeling grief per se. But when I realized that I would never attend another Grateful Dead concert, I got quickly moist, and realized a part of my life was gone forever.

So my colleague asked, "How many have you been to?"

"Over three hundred," I replied, beginning to mist up, "but that wasn't enough."

SCOTT CASSEDAY

For the past thirty years, at every major turning point in my life, the music was always there. Like an old friend who just happens to show up at the right time. My first high, first love, first heartbreak, my marriage, and the birth of my children—there was always a Dead tune to match the mood or situation. The music could bring me up, bring me down, or help in those contemplative times. It's very hard to put into words the power that music has over one. I can say without reservation that the first show I saw in the summer of 1965 shaped the way I deal with people and situations. Maybe the crowd had something to do with it, maybe the city, but the music definitely made an impression that is still with me today. Going to a show was like seeing old trusted friends. An outdoor show was the only show that I would even think about taking my children to.

I'm a grown man, highly educated with a family, and a respected member of my community. I cried off and on for two days when I heard of his death. It was as if

something inside of me too had died. I never joined the circus and followed the band but managed to see them whenever they were in the Bay Area. And I saved all of my ticket stubs. Going through them the other day was like going through letters from an old lover. Wonderful, happy memories came back to me. But where there were once smiles, only tears came. I could always count on the fact that if I didn't get to see them in the spring tour, I'd catch them for sure in the fall. Just like clockwork.

A long chapter in my life has come to a close. It's still hard to believe that it's over. But I have my memories and we have the music. Jerry's music will always touch me the way that it always has, but there will forever be a sadness to it now.

The Captain has come home to rest. Godspeed, my old friend. You will be missed for a long, long time. Thank you.

I will survive.

KEITH KARRAKER

I know the Dead didn't invent jamming, or the sixties, and that their fans aren't the only group of people that allow themselves to be taken over by the collective unconsciousness of a good show. I know my life will still be filled with enjoyable moments. I ain't obsessed, man.

But I'm saying that that tribe, that society, that aura of what was going on is not going to be together in the same way anymore. I know that a lot of heads will be at every Phish show now, and that Haight Street will still be clogged with dirty rat-haired misfits, and the middle of the pit at a Ramones or Mike Watt show will still provide the group synergy, but it ain't gonna be the same as seeing the fat man belting out "Standing on the Moon" with my pumpkin hugging me and the stars in the sky above us. That's all.

DANIEL MARCUS

I've been in a state of mild numbness ever since I heard the news this morning. I've never been a real Deadhead, never even been to a GD show, but their music has been a touchstone for me in a fundamental way for some twenty-five years. I was driving down the wide, flat streets of Livermore during lunch today, looking for a place to get a key copied, and "Box of Rain" came on the radio. I just started crying—surprised the hell out

of me. Coasting through Leave-It-To-Beaver land with the hot sun beating down on the roof of my car, filled with loss. I remember one steamy languid afternoon with a young woman named Jenny in her East Village apartment the summer *American Beauty* came out, making love all afternoon and playing that record over and over. Sweet, sweet memories. And I think of those memories of mine multiplied by all the people with similar heart-connections to that music, and it is just astonishing. Good-bye, Jerry, and thanks. You left a lot of happiness behind you.

RITA HURAULT

Although Disneyland bills itself as "The Happiest Place on Earth," in my experience (and I loved Disneyland), a Dead show was always exactly that, a place where thousands of people gathered with big smiles on their faces and clothed in ways to please themselves and others, happy down to their souls. I have to think that the energy of that

has been good for the planet, and I am grateful I got to be part of it a little while, and grieve at the loss of the music and the experience.

MICHAEL NEWMAN

Garcia was a risk-taker. From Garcia and the Dead, I learned that creative endeavor fulfills me when I sharpen my skills and open myself to meet the moment, rather than rehearse a preconception of how an event should unfold.

KATHY WATKINS

One of my favorite moments was at Telluride. The band had started to play "Brokedown Palace" and it wasn't sounding good. Jerry walked up to the mike and said, "Wait a minute! This is all fucked up—it's in a different key." He chuckled, and they stopped and restarted the song.

There was something about that moment that really stuck with me. It was such a human thing to do. So casual, so mellow. I meditated on the word mellow for the rest of the show and for days after. If you could be that mellow playing in front of thousands of people, you could be mellow anywhere, any time. You could just constantly be mellow.

WARFIELD THEATER, SAN FRANCISCO, 1980
RICHARD McCAFFREY

For some strange reason this was a big breakthrough for me, and I stopped being such a stress puppy and started trying to practice the art of mellow.

I'm still working on it.

ELAINE RICHARDS

I never noticed the GD, much. Just for grins one day, I got a couple of CDs at Costco. I had such a good laugh when I realized that I recognized all the tunes from my childhood. I was about ten in 1966 and the GD got a lot of airplay on the radio in NYC. I actually did go to a concert at the Frost outside. I had just eaten, it was warm, I was tired, I took a nap. Oh well. At least I felt comfortable enough to lie down on the grass in the middle of a huge crowd of people. It was not as compelling to me as to others, but it was nice and we need more niceness.

AL GIORDANO

I remember, vividly, the September 5, 1989, Jerry Garcia Band show at the Hartford Civic Center.

I had been a journalist for one year, and was working my first staff writer job at a western Massachusetts news and arts weekly. That was the night that George Bush was making his "War on Drugs" speech on national TV (where he waved the little bag of crack that was seized from a kid the DEA lured to the park across from the White House).

I was very bothered that day, before the show. The aged district attorney in Springfield, Mass. was trying to intimidate me at the time. This was a guy who played racquetball with the local mafia boss and dispensed "justice" as a series of personal vendettas. Today, six years later, I'll admit that I was really frightened of this DA, and frightened about the escalation of the drug war under way.

Jerry began the second set with Jimmy Cliff's "The Harder they Come," singing how he'd rather die a free man than live out his life as a slave.

The image of that DA, a thirty-two-year incumbent, flooded my head. Seeing and hearing Jerry up there I thought, "I will not be afraid." It was clear to me that Garcia had been fearless for a quarter century, in the face of arrests and censorship. Well, I dunno, maybe it was the "roses," but I suddenly knew that this DA could be brought down, and found a new confidence that I could deliver him that fate.

Returning to work the next day, I set about investigating and writing, over the next

KEN KESEY CLOSING WINTERLAND, DECEMBER 31, 1978
RICHARD McCAFFREY

year, more than twenty major stories about this guy and his abuses of power. By the following summer, the DA had been censured by the state Board of Bar Overseers (for trying to pressure a judge on behalf of an organized crime defendant), and Ryan left office in disgrace.

So, to Jerry I owe a very tangible debt. He infused me with a fearlessness that was mixed with sweetness. He was a direct catalyst for the series of events that made my career, not to mention perhaps preserving my freedom.

I've never written this story down before today. I've probably only told it to a half-dozen people. While the Dead were still touring with Jerry, I worried that a story like this might bring additional heat upon the GD scene. There was always that fine line to be walked between telling the whole truth about the adversarial revolutionary relationship of the Grateful Dead to the dominator culture that rules this land, and the need to keep certain truths unspoken.

Now it can be told. Wave that flag, wave it wide and high. I'll bet that many other Deadheads have similar stories of bizarrely concrete results on the outside world that were born of their music.

KEN KESEY

Jerry Garcia was a great warrior, battling for hearts and souls way out on a dangerous frontier.

The Dire Wolf finally got him.

MARY BUFFINGTON

I still can't quite believe he's gone.

I came to the Dead as a very fucked-up kid over half a lifetime ago. I came to like myself through the Dead. This music—always the Jerry tunes—was able to touch and regenerate a heart turned to stone a long time prior.

I can speak much to the sadness for the passing of a man I only knew through his music. How do you explain a gaping hole in the heart for a man you had no "real" personal, face-to-face relationship with? How is it that there seems to be this big hole in the universe? Its not like I'll miss coffee with him in the morning or talking to him on the phone or telling him what's happening in my life.

I still feel like I've lost a good friend, though.

I can understand and talk about the loss of something larger than Jerry: the Grateful Dead. When will I ever feel that joy, that loss of self, that connection to the whole again? Where will this community of people be drawn and recreated from? How will it renew itself? This may be terribly selfish, but what will become of us?

Maybe the band will resurrect and mutate. But it won't be the same music without Garcia's humility and warm, generous spirit shining through those warbled guitar notes. The difference in the band after Pigpen died was tremendous. The gap with the loss of Brent was huge. Garcia takes another huge chunk of the warmth of the Dead with him.

There is a sweetness, a pathos, a love to Jerryness that isn't found in Phil's thundering bass or Bobby's electricity-crackling rhythm playing. Perhaps its the nature of the roles in the ensemble—the lead guitar being the more emotionally expressive instrument—but I think it's also the heart of each musician. Garcia's heart and soul blazed simply through his music as big as the sun. It was his gift.

Garcia was a lot of the love in the Grateful Dead.

JERRY AND DONNA GODCHAUX CLOSING WINTERLAND, JANUARY 1, 1979
RICHARD McCAFFREY

E L I Z A B E T H   F O X

This may sound trivial, but one thing I've thought of today—I am no longer taking any crap from anyone about liking the Dead and their music. So many of my friends are ex-Deadheads who now hate the whole scene, or others who have contempt for it. I'm neutral about the tie-dye and the painted vans—that's not what it's about for me. But the music is a part of my life, and I'm not going to take crap for that any more.

Because if I hadn't been so apologetic, I might have gotten to see them once. Now I'll never get to, and I'm sorry. I treasure the music more for that.

M A R K   S A L T V E I T

The reasons for hating the band and its crowds are not so much for the music, it's the obnoxious religious bliss of fans who won't listen to anything else despite all evidence of lameness in current music, and the mooching behavior of upper-middle-class fans thrilling to pretend they are poor Kerouac-like drifters.

Like the old joke: "How do you know if your roommate had Deadheads staying over? Because they're still here."

I remember partying with some Deadheads back in high school at a speech tournament, an all-nighter in a motel room with a tape deck, and we nearly had to come to blows to get the Deadheads to play ANY other band—and then, they would only settle for Santana. It just gets fucking rude.

There was some genuine nice feeling among those crowds, but there are also a lot of very affluent people justifying their corporate suburban life by giving a stranger an apple or a joint at a concert and anointing themselves as pure.

At least Nirvana fans don't tell you that you don't "get it" or can't appreciate the "truly special people" they met at concerts. Dead shows seemed like an open party all right, but more like college—a normal selection of people (except more affluent) temporarily suspending their social regulations.

S T E V E   S I L B E R M A N

The woman at CNN asked me if I "dressed like a Deadhead."
I said, "Yes. I wear whatever I want."

L E W I   L O N G M I R E

It's kind of funny, you know? I really hadn't planned on going to any shows anytime soon (money's funny!) and actually was kind of burned out on the boys a bit . . . but now! I feel like I went back to my home town and found out they tore down the house I grew up in and built a parking lot! Jerry split with a part of my growing up, and now I feel trapped in some kinda adulthood!

G A R Y   G R E E N B E R G

Today is the third day of the rest of my life. Since noon on Wednesday, when the news of Jerry Garcia's death began to flash around the world, I have had to grapple with what it means to come to the end of one of the most significant adventures I have ever had. Mine was a long ride on the bus, lasting over twenty years. I had been preparing myself for this moment for quite a while now, particularly as Garcia's decline accelerated in recent years. But, in the end, there is only so much preparation one can make for an event as momentous and unwelcome as this one, only so much insurance one can take out against grief.

In these three days, many people have reached out to console me. I have had anguished, tearful conversations with other members of the polyglot tribe known as Deadheads. And, to my surprise, friends, family, colleagues, and clients—people who have no first-hand experience of the Grateful Dead, but who know of my allegiance— have called or come by just to see how I was doing.

All of this is undoubtedly recognizable to anyone who has had a death in the family. At such times, our loneliness and need are more crucial than our independence, so our unity takes precedence over our separateness. The boundaries in which we live our little lives loosen up, and we are immersed in the warmth of human kindness.

But Jerry Garcia was not a member of my family; I didn't even know him, at least not in the usual sense of the word. Perhaps it seems foolish that I—an educated professional approaching mid-life—would feel my life's foundations rocked by this death. After all, as Garcia himself was so fond of reminding us, he was just a musician.

But a Dead show was not just a concert. It was a place of worship. The band was the high priest, the songs the liturgy, the dancing the prayer, the audience the congregation. Out of these simple ingredients, we created a tradition and enacted a ritual that

was at once entirely familiar and thoroughly mysterious. And often, if not always, we were party to what is, in our particular social and political world, a miracle. Thousands of people gathered together to do precisely what we cannot do in most public places: be open, vulnerable, and trusting of one another, shed the isolation and alienation thrust upon us by our increasingly franchised and commodified world, bask in the simple glory of human love.

For a moment we could be free of corporate logos, of the bank accounts and name brands that we measure ourselves and each other by, of the petty strivings that keep us locked in our isolated selves. For a moment, we could be swept up in something bigger than all of us, something that reached out across the darkness and carried us away to a place rarely seen and more obscured every day. For a moment, we could be our best selves, people for whom all that really mattered was the joy of everyone else, who knew that only their ecstasy was our own. And in those moments of perfect Grateful Deadness, we collectively stormed the gates of heaven, entered a sacred chamber of the universe from which we returned, always reluctantly, always transformed.

At the wheel of the ship, leading the charge in his gentle and unassuming way, was Jerry Garcia. With a voice as warm as a creaking floorboard and as comfortable as the

old leather shoe that walks on it, playing guitar like a spider weaves a web, he spun out story after story about that place. His simple and breathtakingly pure improvised melodies helped to clear away the deadening detritus that keeps us apart. He was like a guide in the jungle, wielding his guitar like a machete, clearing new paths to that corner of the cosmos.

There are other gates to other sacred places. But this one door, this one that I have gone through regularly for twenty-three years, is closed forever. The place that lies behind it will stand forever dark and empty. I will never visit it again, and my life will always be impoverished for this loss.

BILL GRAHAM AND GRATEFUL DEAD, SAN FRANCISCO, DECEMBER 31, 1982
RICHARD McCAFFREY

It is remarkable that something so powerful hinges on something so fragile as the heartbeat of a single, fragile man. Perhaps I am foolish to have hitched my wagon to this particular comet. But, as Jerry Garcia sang so many times, "It all rolls into one. And nothing comes for free. There's nothing you can hold for very long." I am lucky to have found out how true this is.

RICH AND ROBIN ZWEIBACK

Having the Dead come to town two or three times a year was like having Christmas come. The whole anticipation of awaiting the mail-order date, awaiting the tickets, getting that yellow slip in your mailbox, the post office wait, and finally opening the envelope with your tickets was to me much like the whole Xmas ritual. Of course then comes the count-off to the show, the parking-lot party, and finally, the show.

The whole Dead experience was like Santa Claus coming to town.

I never thought Santa Claus could die.

BRUCE KATZ

I was thousands of miles away when Jerry died, but as fate would have it I heard of his death thirty minutes after it was announced. It cast a deep shadow over the day and for the next few days my friends and I talked about what the Dead meant to us. Being the oldest person around, and having lived in my truck in the Haight in the summer of 1969, it had quite a different meaning to me.

My first reaction was the sixties are over—a sentiment I would later find out was widely expressed. But as I thought about it for the next days I realized that what I had found in going to Dead concerts for the last three years was that my feeling in discovering the community of the Deadheads is that the sixties somehow survived and is being continually renewed in this extended family of this very talented and endearing band. I have made many wonderful new friends over the last years around the Dead and have taken my seventy-five-year-old parents to the Oakland Coliseum to stand for three hours and dance in the bleachers.

I am saddened by Jerry's departure, and especially since he had so many good years to go. I never knew him personally but I hope that he moved on from us with peace of mind and a deep understanding of how much he did for so many of us.

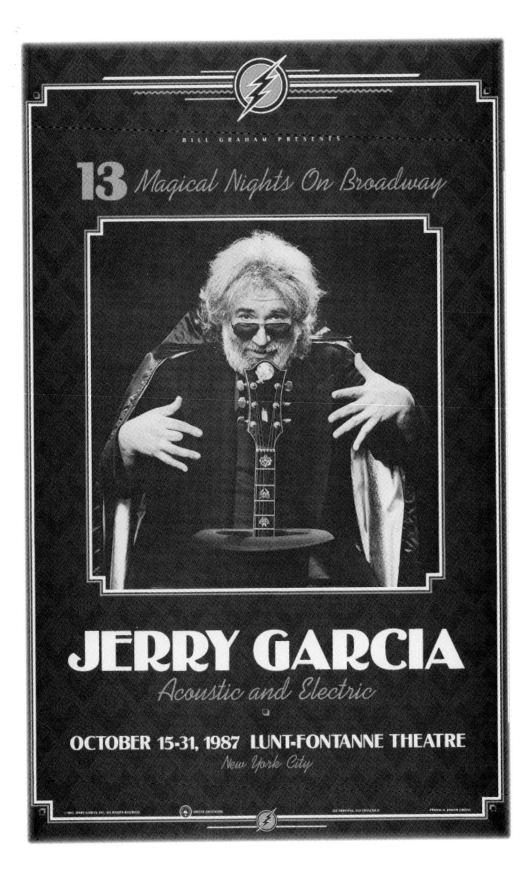

So in the end, I believe the unity of mankind and the knowing of how close we can be with so many is something that goes on with all of us. What we learned in the sixties we can't ever forget. Sometimes it is hard to live in this world and to live by those high and idealistic values that we found there and at the concerts, but we can never really get them out of our guts.

It is up to us to carry the torch of what we have learned from Jerry and the community of which, through him, we became a part. We will all meet again, and I for one will not forget the spirit of what he gave to us.

TIM MILLER

I first saw the Dead in the fall of 1970 in Cleveland. I never became a "tour-follower," but they changed my view of life forever. The main thing is the music itself, of course, but there's more than that—when I first saw them, I was very insecure with my place in the universe. They told me, "It's OK. The universe is a basically friendly place. Shit happens, yes, but in the big scheme of things everything is just as it's supposed to be." This love affair has had one frustrating aspect: one can never communicate to those who have not yet "got it" how important it is, and why.

The Grateful Dead will always be a part of me.

ROGER HUNTER

He was a friend of mine. And of yours. And maybe of your neighbor. And maybe of your classmate or co-worker, or postman, or . . . well, you get the idea. We are everywhere. We all have a commonality in having been touched by this thing called the Grateful Dead. If the highest purpose of art is to transform, who among us hasn't been transformed substantially by the Grateful Dead experience. I'm sure I'm not alone when I say that the Grateful Dead changed my life, that every time I catch a show, I thank whoever needs to be thanked that this life-enriching experience exists and I think that this would be a nice way to spend every day. And however self-deprecating Jerry was about being perceived as any kind of icon, the fact is that for me, and I'm sure for many others, Jerry was a spiritual leader in our attempt to lay a higher consciousness over much of our mundane lives.

Our time on this earth is short. In Jerry's fifty-three years on this planet, he affected

millions of people with his unconditional love. And that love was returned to him and to the rest of the band every time they played, every time any one of us listened to a tape, every time any of us saw another Deadhead in the unlikeliest of places. For that amount of positive energy to have been created and sustained for three generations is unbelievable. But we believe it. Because we know it. Because we were there. And now we have to decide if it really is worth carrying on. I hope it is. I think Jerry would be real pissed if there was a chance that his passing meant the end of what he helped to create. We need to mourn in our own way/faith, but we also need to celebrate his legacy—a legacy that lives in the memory that all us have of every show, every love-filled thought, every crazy incident, every time we met a lifelong companion, every time we laughed, every time we had a magical moment, every time . . .

There is a saying that we don't die as long as one person remembers us. I remember the Fox Theater in St. Louis. I remember Des Moines. I remember Telluride. I remember

Alpine Valley, Shoreline, Eugene, Oakland, the Greeks, and countless others. I remember the second set of July 9th, when Phil commandeered the microphone to indicate that he was going to sing "Box of Rain." "Such a long, long time to be gone/ And a short time to be there." Having sung an unprecedented three songs that night, Phil was still standing at the mic, guitar poised, the last one to leave the stage. I'll always remember the way he looked over as his eyes followed a departing Jerry. And I'll always remember Jerry. Love is real . . . Not Fade Away . . . Because some things are forever . . .

D A N   L E V Y

I was never in the "Jerry is God" camp. As much as the Dead have meant to me, I never, even when I was a kid, thought of the Dead as rock stars, to be worshiped from afar. They're working musicians, playing ever-bigger dance halls.

Grateful Dead shows, on the other hand, were my sacred festivals, and the special ones my High Holy Days. I've found myself reaching out to the people who I met at Dead concerts, the friends I might never have made without showing up for one more night of dancing and letting the music get me high. Some are people I may never run into again, some have become lifelong friends.

We'll always have those great times we had together. Now it's time to take the best that being a Deadhead has to offer and make the world shine with the love and misfit power and the sheer affirmation of creativity and improvisation that the Dead have always tried to express in their music and their style of business.

S T E V E   B A R N C A R D

Jerry was a working associate and inspiration to me in the three or four years I had the pleasure of working with him—on *American Beauty*, the first New Riders record, Crosby's first solo record, *Blows Against the Empire*, and those informal Planet Earth Rock 'n' Roll Orchestra Sessions—and always anticipated his arrival at the studio, for a session with Jerry was like nothing else. His humor and great vibes and playing always

combined to make a fun and magic session. He once pronounced in the studio: "God invented the night . . . for recording!!!"

Jer, we miss you.

S T E V E   S I L B E R M A N

Garcia: A Craftsman, Not An Icon

The last time I saw Jerry Garcia up close was backstage at the Cal Expo Amphitheater in Sacramento, on one of those sun-saturated afternoons when families from all over the Bay Area would turn a Dead show into a picnic for all ages. The witty, self-deprecating guitarist—who had become increasingly reclusive under the burden of being an icon—paused on the steps leading up to the stage to sign autographs for a group of kids who clustered around him.

Jewish friends of mine used to joke that the Dead's annual concerts at the Greek Theater in Berkeley were the real High Holy Days. You'd see the same faces year after year—with a few more gray hairs, or a new wedding ring—mixed in with those of fresh-faced kids who always seemed to find the Dead's excursions into the unknown relevant, generation after generation. Those concerts at the Greek often took place over a three-day stretch, with the middle show commencing in daylight, and ending in darkness. At dusk, with the full face of the moon rising behind the glittering towers of San Francisco, there was no place on Earth a Deadhead would rather have been.

When the Dead made headlines this past summer, it was the tragic lightning-strikes and gate-crashing fans that were cast in the starring roles, rather than the music. The fact that the Dead kept up a conversation in song for three decades—a quintessentially American synthesis of jazz, folk balladry, avant-garde soundscapes, transcultural rhythmatism, and good ol' time rock-and-roll redemption—took the back seat. That the only accomplishment of comparable longevity in exploratory American music-making was, say, Duke Ellington's Orchestra, was barely acknowledged.

Garcia once quipped that the Dead, like old whores and bad architecture, simply stuck around long enough to become respectable. They did more than that. They managed to become the most financially successful touring rock-and-roll band in history without caving into industry homogenization or type-casting as a "sixties band," and without distilling the dissonant and unpredictable edge out of their music. At nearly every show, there was still one moment of pure discovery, a jam that went somewhere it had

never been before (and never would be again), an emotional peak which seemed to boil up out of some primordial storehouse.

During those breakthrough moments, when a vitality beyond words momentarily banished the woes of the world, the teenagers and the grizzled older folks would turn to one another in a shared moment of recognition. When "the music played the band," as the song says, even the stars shimmering in the indigo sky above the Golden Gate seemed to be part of the tune. And through it all, the collective body of Deadheads danced, poised on the brink of a mystery.

Garcia himself never claimed to be captain of anybody's trip but his own, and it must have irked him a little to see his face plastered on bumper stickers and t-shirts. "It's bad enough," Garcia once joked to a friend of mine, "that my face turns up on my head every morning."

I weep today, knowing that after twenty-two years of seeing him play—at places like the Greek and the Frost and the Kaiser Auditorium, and local clubs like the Keystone— I will never again be able to look up onstage, and witness the focused emotions of a craftsman, wholly absorbed in his craft, crossing that whiskered face that I came to love.

INTERNATIONAL CONGRESS CENTRUM, BERLIN, GERMANY, OCT. 20, 1990
JOHN ROTTET

I saw that keen earnestness that afternoon in the sun at Cal Expo, as Garcia scribbled his name on napkins and ticket stubs, for the little ones eager for a souvenir of the man who expressed the secret music of our hearts. After signing a couple of dozen, he looked up, and suddenly noticed how large the crowd of kids waving scraps of paper toward him had grown.

Garcia gave a little shrug of exaggerated horror for his own amusement, like the look W. C. Fields gives the hapless Mr. Muckle when he crashes through the window of Fields' grocery store in *It's A Gift*. Then Garcia reached into the crowd again, brought the next scrap of paper up close, and went back to work.

Op-ed piece in the San Francisco Chronicle, August 11, 1995

STEWART BRAND

Interesting how "Uncle John's Band" seems to have become the anthem of choice on the radio.

. . . what I want to know/ is are you kind?

I can't think of anyone kinder than Jerry Garcia. His kindness reached as far as his music, touched and turned generations.

DAVID GRISMAN

Jerry and I were friends for over thirty years. It's impossible to put into words the profound impact that he had on my life, both musically and spiritually. His love for and commitment to good music of all kinds was one hundred percent. I'm honored and privileged to have known him and shared so many wonderful moments. As one of his thousands of admirers, I will miss him deeply. Good-bye, old pal.

HENRY KAISER

I did not start playing guitar until the middle of my college years in 1972. By that time I had been exposed to the Grateful Dead, in concert and on record, for six years. I think a lot of my musical and socio-musical values developed from unconsciously emulating the Dead, who were probably my favorite band.

Let me list what I perceive those values to be in 1995:

1) Improvisation produces the best music. It connects creation with the present moment and the audience both past, present, and future.

2) Take chances! Push yourself and your collaborators. Experimental music is often the best music. Be original. Create your own personal voice. (As Carlos Santana once said: "Your grandmother should be able to recognize you even if you only play one note.")

3) Playing music together is about people: your collaborators and your audience. Try to work together in a cooperative way that will make the whole bigger than the sum of the parts.

4) Be inquisitive and eclectic. Look to all the musics and musical idioms of planet earth to inform and influence yourself. Jazz, Country, Blues, Experimental, Classical, etc. etc. etc. everything from everywhere.

5) As Albert Ayler so eloquently expressed: "Music is not about notes, it's about feelings."

6) As I heard Jerry say several times: "I serve the music." This is the best attitude, I think. This sums it up: Serve The Music.

To me that's the most important thing I learned from Jerry. His life was about it. Serve the music. And I think that by serving the music—you end up serving people. Jerry did more for more human beings than anyone else I have ever known personally. I think our job is to continue his service to music and people. To quote Robert Hunter from "Mason's Children":

> **Mason was a mighty man**
> **A mighty man was he**
> **All he said: "When I'm dead and gone**
> **don't you weep for me."**

JUDE MCDONALD

[Jerry will be reincarnated] as a long string of notes, truly whole notes, spherical bouncing balls of inspiration, bent and twisted notes with glints of electric lightning shooting out across the deep unreal, rising and rising until a song catches on the edge of chaos . . . forever and ever.

JON HOFFMAN

Jerry was the binding glue and opening force that connected the hearts of thousands of people in ways that we never knew were possible. Within the constraints

of our human forms we have had a taste of the eternal and infinite. More importantly, Jerry was one of us—he did not want to be in the role of god, leader, or Buddha. He was very human, and cared more about the music and all of us than himself. We will miss him forever, but will also feel forever the good fortune, and thanks for the blessings that have fallen our way. Hang in there and keep the flame burning with everyone you ever meet. We are all here to help each other through this human condition—glimpses of reality, but stuck in this impermanent world.

STEVE SILBERMAN

I now understand the Wailing Wall a little better, having visited three shrines dedicated to Garcia—one in the Fillmore, one at Haight and Ashbury, and one at the Fillmore East.   The coolest thing on any of the altars that I saw was a sign on the one at Haight that had been pirated from a Muni bus. It read:

Sudden Stops necessary
Please hold on

GREENSBORO COLISEUM, NC, MARCH 30, 1989
JOHN ROTTET

DRUMS AND SPACE

Now he's gone
And gone too the blessing of his
presence
Gone the plain spontaneity
Gone the delicate elegance
Gone the lunatic doodlings
Gone the miraculous bastions
Gone the manic placid dance
Gone the mystical candor
Gone the transcendental intensity
Gone the naughty raucous chaos
Gone the haunting lostness
Gone the heady impressions
Gone the festive message
Gone the trippy sinful gist
Gone the grumpy uncle
Gone the happy rabbi
Gone the moody Buddha
Gone the sly smiling Santa
Gone the complex knowledge
Gone the all things possible
Gone the honest promise
Gone the future evolutions
Gone the future forever
Gone
Gone with pallid finality
He's gone and nothing's going
to bring him back
No nothing's left but drums
and space

9 August 1995

Our sadness and our gratitude at last
But if the purpose of the journey
Is the journey to a purpose
The inevitable end of everything
Then go Jerry

Go off to your next destiny
Go away engaged in the great
translation
Go take your place on the playground
Go find all your old friends
Go spawn the long forgotten
Go spread the best epic yet
Go track the everlasting vastness
Go watch it all happen
Go to it
Go be who you are
(Like you always taught us
Like the essence of your lesson
ever:
Be who you are)
Yes go be who you are
The rehearsal is over
Go jam a stratospheric passage
Go blow the most heroic solos
Until nothing's left but drums
and space

Shred the heavens man
We'll be listening for you

A MANDALA

By the time we have become adults, most of us have learned to let most things roll off our backs pretty quickly so we can keep on keeping on. But for each of us there are still those few things that easily pierce that armor and tear at our souls and losing Jerry is just such a wound to my core. Hearing Jerry play was the one balm that could always soothe all my ills, and his passing has left me both with the worst ill ever and no way to soothe it away. On the whole, life is still sweet, but I've never tasted so much bitter pain and sadness before and it's totally overwhelming at times.

But when I find myself drowning in that sorrow, I try to remember that it is a feeling

POTRERO HILL, SAN FRANCISCO, 1968
MALCOLM LUBLINER

I share only with my Deadhead sisters and brothers left behind. I remind myself of that smile Jerry left on his face and my heart warms that he found "a little peace to die" especially after all the difficulty he seemed to have during the last year or so. And then I think about the reports that when we cross over we are reunited with those we love who have gone before, and I imagine that maybe that smile on that face of one who'd served as a happy father for so many was from that little Jerry Garcia who was finally reunited with his own father whom he'd had to watch drown and leave him when he was only a five-year-old-kid. Most of all, I've always wished for Jerry that he had something to make him as happy as his music made me, and even though I'm sad that he had to leave this world to find it, I'm glad he found it in the end.

"Lay down my dear brother, lay down and take your rest." And enjoy dreaming those dreams and singing those songs of your own . . .

GARY GREENBERG

The Sunday after Jerry died, I had to shoot and kill a cat. I love cats, and I hate killing anything, but it was a feral cat that was terrorizing our cats and had staked out our front porch as its territory. I did the deed, cleanly, and buried the cat, and then just sat down and stared into the air. I was too demoralized even to cry. Death's mercilessness stalked the land, seemed to have settled in for a long stay.

The next night I had the following dream. I was at a Dead show at Madison Square Garden, sitting in the seats that I had gotten for one of the upcoming fall shows—back of the floor, Jerry side, my favorite Garden seats. The dream was very un-dreamlike, lacking the usual distortions of time and space, entirely faithful to the details. The band started to play "High Time." In the dream, I was aware of a feeling that had become familiar in recent years: the anxiety that Jerry would falter, forget lyrics, or get tangled in a musical line, as he increasingly had. He sang the first verse, "You told me goodbye. How was I to know you didn't mean goodbye, you meant please don't let me go." Then no more. I tried desperately, as I had on other occasions, to telepath him the words, the music, the will to climb back into the song. But he stopped, and then the band stopped. The Garden breathed with the silence of raw presence, all of us rapt and waiting. Phil and Bob filed off stage left, walking right by Jerry. Left alone, he took off his guitar and a hat he was wearing, and sank down into a half-lotus position. He sat still. Cradled in his arms was a kitten, which he was slowly caressing.

PEALS OF FRAGILE THUNDER

WARFIELD THEATER, SAN FRANCISCO, 1980
RICHARD McCAFFREY

G A R Y   L A M B E R T

. . . that jump-off-the-cliff-and-ask-questions-later kind of recklessness that characterizes the Dead's music at its best . . .

P A T R I C K   R A G A I N S

He had a gentleness and warmth about him that no other "guitar hero" had. He seemed approachable and friendly, as if to say, "Hey, this is no big deal, anyone can do what I do," although, of course, that wasn't true. Certainly he made many people of several generations feel better about themselves, just by playing and being who he was.

D A V I D   G R I S M A N

My Friend Jerry

"Talk to me, David . . . you should talk to me a little bit in my solo . . . ." Garcia was asking me to converse with him musically during the guitar solo he'd be playing after the first verse of "Blue Yodel #9," the Jimmie Rodgers classic, which we had never played together before. "Hi, Jerry, nice solo you're playing," I quipped. We were kidding around, exchanging light-hearted banter like we always did when we got together in the small recording room that used to be my garage.

Decibel Dave slated "Take 1," but after the first verse we stopped, not quite sure whether Garcia would sing a long or short yodel. "The tempo's a little quick, too," Jerry commented. "Down from the bottom brother, say way down from Dixie now," and immediately

MILL VALLEY, CA, APRIL, 1985
f-stop FITZGERALD

kicked off a slower, more laid-back groove. "That's it, that's the feel. Nothing is moving on the river." It had been over a year since Jerry and I had hit any licks together, and this was going to be fun.

Fun was always at the heart of the matter with Jerry, and now, three weeks and a thousand universes later, the notion that my world, and the world of countless others, will be decidedly less fun is painfully settling in. Of course Jerry desperately wouldn't want me or us to feel this way. I'm certain of that. Every fiber of his being was dedicated to the awesome task of making us all feel better, and he always did. He had those special qualities that fused his great creativity with his even greater humanity, tempered always with that sense of humor . . . fun.

Let's not confuse the issue, though. Jerome Garcia was a great leader—musically, morally, and spiritually. He didn't want it, he didn't seek it, he didn't ask for it, he may not have even liked it, but he carried that enormous weight with grace, dignity, and a huge sense of responsibility to his fellow man, particularly those less fortunate. If you needed help, he was there. Of course, as we now know, it was Jerry himself who needed help. And although he was getting it, the years had already taken their toll, and that long strange trip is over.

But is it really over? Not for us — Jerry's kids. We need to take his message to heart and find our own creativity and our own path and help try and make this world a little better, which will be just a little harder for us now. This is our challenge, which I feel we can meet if we can all take a little piece of him with us. We all need to become a little more Jerry-like and move on down the road.

Just one more thing I thought you'd want to know: Jerry died with a smile on his face.

B E R N I E   B I L D M A N

Jerry's playing was like walking past two people talking in a mall. As you pass by, you hear a snippet or two of the conversation and then realize you must quietly stop because you know there is something being said here that shouldn't be missed. Jerry played like that, never asking to be heard but rather sharing freely his musical conversation with anyone who might be interested. The music he played sang notes to the depth of your soul. He was truly a musical alchemist, always searching for the Philosopher's Stone, trying to change lead to gold. There were times that I was certain he had in fact found the Secret. RIP.

PHIL THOMPSON

I don't always get a feeling of structure from other guitarists, but Jerry created rooms and fields that I almost felt I could walk through. He wasn't the fastest or slickest guitarist but he sure could build spaces. He's also the only one that you could identify with one note. One tone and "Ah — Jerry!"

GARY LAMBERT

There were certainly more pyrotechnically dazzling guitarists. There were probably more innovative ones, at least in the area of electronic or stylistically revolutionary developments in the history of the instrument. But there were none more possessed of that rarest of musical qualities: true eloquence. No one on guitar comes close for me, and very few on other instruments. In that almost mystical ability to tell a story without using a single spoken or sung word, there is Lester Young, there is Johnny Hodges, and there is Jerry Garcia. After that, the list is very short.

STEVE SILBERMAN

The "Eyes of the World" from March 29, 1990 (on Without a Net) is a performance for the ages. I would stand it up next to anything by Bach, Miles, anybody. Branford [Marsalis, sitting in on tenor and soprano sax without ever having heard the song before], bless him, is more seamlessly interwoven into the band's fabric than any guest had ever been (Bruce Hornsby was close); and Jerry is just so obviously happy to have a dialogue with a slightly unfamiliar voice as prolifically melodious as his own . . . Listen to the way Jerry plays the bass flute, even (this detail was so meticulous of him it brings tears to my eyes now to think of it) "chuffing" at the end of each breath-phrase the way a flautist would. This whole track could be a lifetime's study for a young guitarist growing up in the MIDI age, of exquisitely subtle and human use of the technology. My favorite part is toward the end, when the band is winding down, and each member of the band starts "singing" to every other member simultaneously, modulating the changes into a darker zone, like a conference of the birds as the great sun sets.

Such a performance ennobles humanity, and makes me think of the brief epitaph Jack Kerouac's wife Stella had cut into his gravestone in Lowell:

He honored life

A L A N   T U R N E R

For group improvisation, there's a lot of bands besides the Dead that do that, and well. Jazz bands and gospel groups come to mind. You can make a good case that the Dead introduced a lot of people to the idea that there is something to music besides a rehearsed-to-death show with scripted spontaneous ejaculations.

O Z   C H I L D S

My first experience was well before their first album, when in a very real way they weren't the musical group they became. Bobby was the real rocker in the band, Pigpen was Mr. Blues, and Jerry was really, really interested in what new sounds he could make with his guitar. For conversion experiences, you had to hear Quicksilver do "Pride of Man" or Big Brother do "Roadblock." Fortunately, Quicksilver, Big Brother, or the Airplane were likely to be on the bill too.

Somewhere around 1968 or 1969, the Dead collectively figured out how to work together as a band — how to combine Lesh's deep musical knowledge, Jerry's exploration, Weir's youth and energy, and the interplay between two drummers into sets that were long conversations, brought to a peak of rock-out excitement near the end. (Sadly, Pigpen became musically irrelevant.) The basic musical problem: How do you get out of "Dark Star" in some way that gets the audience jumping up and down in psychic orgasm? Answer: weave the exploratory lines in such a way that "St. Stephen" or another cathartic song becomes first a possible, then the inevitable solution. And then, when the whole audience thinks that no one could be up for another round, let Bobby lead on a cover of some old rock or R&B standard that is no longer someone else's song, but is something the Dead owned from that moment on.

It must have been amazing to have a concert like that be your first GD experience.

In the summer of 1971, I was living with some buddies from high school and college, in La Jolla (most of us went to UCSD). One day Bob and I were returning from driving up to Del Mar to score a lid, and up on the mesa just north of the campus we saw a hitchhiker with a backpack. As we started to pull over he put his hand to his head and looked skyward in amazement. Turned out he'd just gotten out of a car seconds earlier that had brought him all the way from Big Sur. He must have felt he was in hitchhiking heaven (which San Diego definitely was not).

The hitchhiker's name was Jonathan and he was from London. When we found out he was from another country we immediately "adopted" him, inviting him to crash at our place. We got back to the apartment, introduced him to our roomies, fed him, sampled the freshly acquired herb, and got down to the serious business of entertainment. We were planning to see the Dead that night, so we made a special trip to downtown San Diego to get a ticket for Jonathan. This entire encounter more or less confirmed me on the hippie path.

POTRERO HILL, SAN FRANCISCO, 1968
MALCOLM LUBLINER

I don't remember much about that show (Golden Hall, San Diego, August 7, 1971); one moment that stands out was from an uptempo number (along the lines of "Bertha," but I don't believe it was that song). The band was tearing into the instrumental bridge at a breakneck pace, and there seemed to be some uncertainty as to when to come back to the chorus. Garcia was wailing away, focused on his instrument, on our left; Weir was in the middle, watching him; Lesh on the right, holding down the bottom. As they came up to the moment when they might have ended the bridge, it looked like Garcia wasn't done soloing, but Weir and Lesh were about to launch into vocals. Weir looked at Garcia, and at Lesh, and back at Garcia, and back at Lesh. At the last possible

instant, he shook his head "no" at Lesh. But Lesh was sure they were going to end the jam and resume singing, and continued to move up to the mic. In just that instant, Garcia concluded his solo and stepped up to the mic. Weir had about half a heartbeat to re-re-change direction and begin singing. All three hit the beat and the note/chord thunderously and their voices came in perfectly. It was like an 18-wheeler careening out of control down a mountain road, and the brakes go out, but somehow it manages to avoid a family of ducks crossing the road after a blind curve and continue on its merry way. Still one of the more remarkable, probably the most remarkable, examples of musical derring-do I've ever witnessed.

I didn't know enough of the songs that well to be able to take special pleasure in their doing "favorites," but I was blown away by the power and artfulness of the song-writing and their performance. I came away thoroughly sated, and a believer. I've enjoyed few concerts more.

DAMIAN STRAHL

June 16, 1990, at Shoreline, Jerry was driving the band throughout the entire second set. After "Terrapin," the whole drums/space format had to be abandoned because Garcia insisted on taking everyone through one strange landscape after another. It was thrilling. I can't remember Jerry asserting himself with so much authority for such a long stretch of music. I remember just how quiet the crowd was after the show, drained and awed by his grace and power and creativity.

KATHY WATKINS

When the MIDI stuff started really happening, Jerry seemed to approach it like an exuberant little boy with a great new toy. And then he found the horn sounds. He played trumpet, clarinet, flute, french horn, with the intensity of a diligent new student, and he would find ways to make each of those sounds soar. I loved Jerry as a horn player.

MICHAEL ZENTNER

Jerry was one of those musicians who was able to connect his soul directly into his guitar, and the electric amplification provided by being in a rock'n'roll band let everybody connect right along with him.

STEVE SILBERMAN

There are people who "write poetry," and there are Poets. People who write poetry can work to make two lines rhyme, but a real Poet performs his craft so that people of his age can rhyme with those of ancient times, and rise to acts of heroism worthy of a classical epic in the world as it is.

Likewise, there are people who play music, and Musicians. Jerry Garcia's guitar never lied to you. Where he was at, he played — straight up what's happening, and different every time. There was no bombast, no pose, no "effects": if he felt like hell, he played Hell, or a Heaven so appropriate to just that moment that when you got there, you felt welcomed, like you'd earned it, and all that road dust just fell off you.

Garcia's lifelong commitment to musical scholarship — to hearing clearly the voices that sounded before his own — gave his playing humility, which allowed him that rarest of gifts, in Poets or Musicians: the ability to say, in each and every moment, exactly what needs to be said.

JOHN SIEVERT

You always knew how Jerry felt by the way he was playing on any given night. He had plenty of technique but never exercised it strictly for its own sake. He studied it like a linguist so he had the "words" to fully express himself.

JON CARROLL

I have to say that I met Jerry Garcia once and that he did not make much of an impression on me. It was mid-afternoon; he had been up for perhaps an hour; he drank a Bud and talked mostly about the implicit politics of the Dead, which is mostly what I asked him about. I knew so little about him that I was surprised when I noticed his runcated finger. He seemed charmed by the fact that I was surprised.

There was a time in my life, though, a time perhaps two years before I interviewed Jerry Garcia, that the album *American Beauty* served for me as a kind of life raft. I was very very afraid — afraid of losing my children; afraid of going crazy — and only a few things on earth could begin to restore me to sanity. One was the sight of white deer standing in the tall bushes at the edge of a pine forest on Pt. Reyes. Another was *American Beauty* which, like *Music From Big Pink*, struck me as a gift and a promise. It

was the door that opened just a crack; through it I could see the light beyond.

I never mentioned that to him; I wouldn't have known where to begin.

RICHARD GEHR

To Lay Him Down

Three days since Jerry Garcia's untimely finale in the bucolic-sounding Serenity Knolls rehab center, and I'm still shambling through a suddenly less interesting world. Garcia and lyricist Robert Hunter's "Standing on the Moon" won't leave my head. "A lovely view of heaven, but I'd rather be with you," howled Garcia during his last year onstage — the song's concluding lyric yet another chiming affirmation of the Grateful Dead's limitlessly complex and ambivalent relationship with its audience (though, as with all Hunter songs, interpretive mileage varies considerably). I'm somewhere in the Catskills, ostensibly on vacation, detached from the media clusterfuck, unable to hear the Dead's music even if I could stand to, and writing shivas as the wind whispers sweet farewells through the rich August foliage. But Friday night, after a couple of hits of some

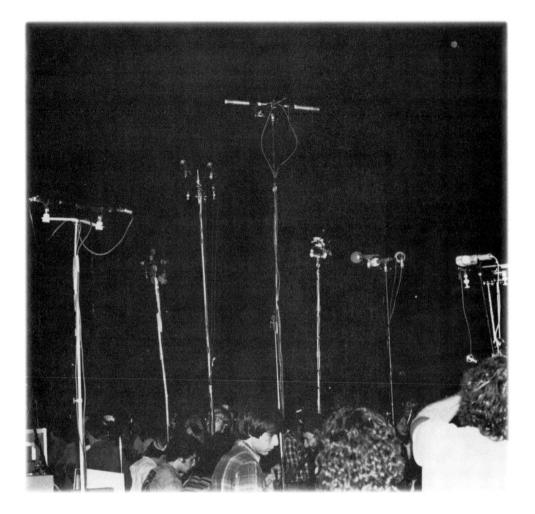

occasional hash, I spontaneously flick the dial of a radio tuned, as usual, to the world's only hydroelectrically powered public radio station. Tears fall one more time as the opening chords of — what else?—"Standing on the Moon" chime like church bells through the boombox.

No matter from which direction you choose to engage or deny them, Jerome John Garcia and the Grateful Dead mirrorballed nearly everything exciting and important about American music of the past three decades. The only reasonably comparable musical legacy is the Duke Ellington Orchestra, to whom Garcia/Hunter offered musical homage in "Mississippi Halfstep Uptown Toodeloo." Garcia developed an ever-evolving musical palette that connected Earl Scruggs, Django Reinhardt, Chuck Berry, and Ornette Coleman. Yet his solos — rambling guitar narratives of mythical scale, lyrical wit, and emotional risk — always bore his immediately recognizable signature, warm and earthy phrases as subtly alien as his right paw print.

OAKLAND AUDITORIUM, DECEMBER 31, 1979
RICHARD McCAFFREY

Last of the beats and first of the hippies, Garcia ascended from the hootenanny into the starship before falling back to earth. In a sense, every Dead show traced that same hazardous arc. From the humble beginnings of a warmup set focusing mainly on roots music, the perennially avant-garde combo would spiral collectively skyward toward the dark nova of the second set's freely improvised drums/space centerpiece before returning to one of Garcia's redemptive epiphanies and an R&B eruption. Fact is, give or take a "Dark Star," no band ever played so much freely improvised music to so large an audience as the Grateful Dead, which is to say that no band ever took so many musical risks night after night, tour after tour, year after year, generation after generation.

I was an ignorant young stoner the first time I saw the Dead. But it didn't take me long to realize that a Dead show could be far more than a party — in fact, it was the closest thing to a holy communion I might ever know. After attaining a semblance of adulthood, I saw shows as strange, celebratory hybrids of picnics, baseball games, and revival meetings. And maybe every show in three, the secrets would be revealed in all their crazy splendor and it would once again feel like nothing less than a modern version of the ancient Greeks' Eleusinian mystery rites.

Problem was, nobody asked Garcia if he wanted to be the tragic high priest of this religion cum circus. Likewise, how could he have avoided it? His youthful music vibrates with all the freedom and potential the sixties had to offer. Unfortunately, Garcia's personal karma seems to have stalled somewhere in the seventies and eighties, decades whose indulgences and delights drew many into their jaded riptide maw. In the end, Garcia was just a man, a craftsman more than a symbol, tragically incapable of basking in the beauty he regularly delivered to his audience. Where Frank Zappa lived in constant fear of his music being stolen, Garcia gave his away freely to the tapers, creating the largest, publicly documented musical legacy in musical history. Say what you want about his chops, Garcia died with the stats.

It's difficult to imagine another contemporary musician transforming the landscape of American music with as quicksilver an alchemy as Garcia. As much chemical substance as pop star, he turned the subject-object relationship of listener and artist upside-down, reflecting back each auditor's best self in an impossibly bemused and knowing voice, and guitar notes as dear as precious metal. He was an Armstrong, a Coltrane, a Miles . . . a Garcia.

12 August 1995

HIS JOB
IS
TO SHED
LIGHT

GIANTS STADIUM, NEW JERSEY, JUNE 19, 1995
PHILIP ANDELMAN

G A R Y   L A M B E R T

In July of 1969 the Grateful Dead played two hastily booked, little-publicized concerts at what had been the New York State Pavilion, a wonderful open-air structure
designed by Philip Johnson for the 1964-'65 World's Fair at Flushing Meadows, in the
fair borough of Queens. The band's shows at the Pavilion coincided with one of the most
wildly hyped events of the late sixties: the American debut, at Madison Square Garden,
of the first so-called supergroup, Blind Faith. Garcia, from the stage, wondered aloud
what the fuck anyone was doing at his humble little band's show when they could be off
seeing the rock demigods on display at the Garden. The Dead then proceeded to remind
us what the fuck we were doing there, by playing what was without a doubt the best

POTRERO HILL, SAN FRANCISCO, 1968
MALCOLM LUBLINER

rock show I had heard in my life to that point (and it remains high among my peak experiences). At the end of the show, a few folks, myself included, just couldn't bear to tear ourselves away from the place, and bathed in the afterglow by hanging out on the dance floor, which was a giant map of New York State. Suddenly, I was astonished to see Jerry standing a few feet away (somewhere around Syracuse, I think), chatting with some of the audience stragglers. I approached him with some trepidation (my only previous attempt to speak to a "rock star," Al Kooper, had consisted of Kooper brushing past me with a brusque "later, man" before I could get a word out), and said, haltingly, "Uh . . . I just wanted to tell you that that was the most amazing music I've ever heard . . ." To my amazement and delight, Garcia grabbed my right hand in a two-fisted clasp and shook it vigorously, saying, "Hey, thanks a lot, man!! And thanks for comin'!"

It was a wonderfully, demystifying moment. Here was this guy who had been acting as God's own guitar player onstage just moments before, now acting in a decidedly non-iconic, accessible, normal-guy fashion. I'm sure that his openness, enthusiasm, and

GOLDEN GATE PARK, CIRCA 1976
RICHARD McCAFFREY

complete lack of pretense made me a lot more fearless about approaching artists I admired, and treating them not as idols but as regular folks. It was with that new found chutzpah that I started knocking on some of the doors that got me where I am, wherever that is!

B A R R Y   W E L C H

I feel lucky, since I actually met the man several times and found him to be approachable and most cordial. I guess the most meaningful time was once after a show, I asked him if he'd mind signing a picture of him that I'd brought along. No problem, he said and sat down to sign it. I told him it was for my girlfriend at the time (she later became my wife) and he asked what'd I like him to say. I said, "whatever you'd

like, Jerry." He only wrote one word and signed his name. I looked at the picture, looked back at him, and for a brief instant we shared that magical zen-grin feeling that I've always felt whenever he was around. Since that day, any time someone would come around at work asking me to sign a going-away card or picture for someone who was leaving, I just sign it with that single word that Jerry used:

THRIVE!

L I Z A G R O S S

I met Jerry a couple of times and was impressed both times with his graciousness and amazing tolerance of people constantly approaching him. Plus, he was really funny.

The first time I met him was at the Spectrum, April 22,1977. I was sixteen and had drawn this charcoal portrait of him that I wanted to give to him as a small token of my appreciation for all the joy and inspiration that his music had given me. When I gave it to him, he responded in typical Garcia fashion: "What a sorry subject." Unbelievably modest. I had never intended the picture to be any kind of idolization, but just a simple gesture of thanks. I realized later that this was probably just the kind of thing that made him uncomfortable. At the time, though, he couldn't have been more kind or gentle. He really went out of his way to make me feel comfortable, inviting me to hang out there with him and the band until the show started. I'll never forget it.

J E F J A I S U N

There are a lot of things I'll remember fondly about Garcia: the 1968 gig we did outside San Quentin; the Old Fillmore gig after Altamont; the Haight Street gig on the truck (Live Dead insert), after which my old band, The Phoenix, got the overflow crowd in the Straight Theater; being at a Straight gig the first night they brought Mickey out to play with Bill.

But the No. 1 Garcia experience for me happened at 710 [Ashbury] one afternoon in '67. I walked in just to schmooze, and there was Garcia, sitting in a chair and grinning like the cat that just swallowed a canary — playing licks a mile a minute on his new black Les Paul. I watched in awe as he tore that guitar a whole new consciousness. Then he turned to me and said, "This is a great axe, man. Here. Try it!" And he handed me his brand new guitar. He didn't know me from jack, and he handed me his brand new guitar.

PETE GRANT

When I think of Garcia, I think of him unselfishly encouraging and inspiring others, his joy of creation and discovery, and his love of music.

I am deeply saddened by his passing. For him: because he wasn't really done this lifetime. For us: for the same reason.

Before the Grateful Dead or even the Warlocks, Jerry and I were driving in his Corvair up from Palo Alto to Berkeley to see the Kentucky Colonels play. "Together Again" [Buck Owens] came on the radio, with that memorable solo by Tom Brumley. We both listened in reverent awe, and said, "Man, we gotta learn pedal steel." Between the two of us, I was the first to get a steel and start playing, and that's how I ended up playing on *Aoxomoxoa*.

GIANTS STADIUM, NJ, JUNE 19,1995
PHILIP ANDELMAN

When Jerry came back from a tour with a brand new ZB Custom double-10 pedal steel, he absolutely immersed himself in the instrument. I remember going over to his house to see it. He had me playing guitar as soon as I walked in the door, and singing every song I knew, so he could boink around and play backups and solos. Later that day, I showed him some things that I had discovered on the steel, including parts of "Together Again." He got good real fast and had a wonderfully unique style.

About a year later he got another steel, and loaned me the ZB, because the pedal steel I had was quite a clunker. Mine had pedals like a 2-ton truck clutch and knee levers to match. Using the ZB really helped me get a job with my first country band and helped me get good. Later, after I added 3 more knee levers and was playing regularly in a really good country band, I shared my enthusiasm over using the instrument with Jerry. He said, "Well, if you like it that much, I think you ought to keep it." It's a great sounding instrument, and 25 years later, still finds its way into the studio to the delight of recording artists and engineers. And me.

So, today, shortly after I heard the news, I sat down at the ZB, played "Together Again," and played the hell out of it. For Jerry.

Thanks, man. I love you.

KEN SCHUMACHER

I remember a Dead concert at Swing Auditorium in San Bernardino, California, back in 1978. Swing Auditorium was a dirty, airplane hangar type building, located on the Orangefair fairgrounds. Dingy tinsel encrusted with years of accumulated dust hung from the rafters in a feeble attempt to make the hall festive. Although the place was a drab, corndog-and-cotton-candy dive, it warranted a footnote in rock'n'roll history as the first location the Rolling Stones played in the U.S. Alas, the Swing no longer stands because some errant pilot crashed his private plane directly into the building, killing himself and causing enough structural damage to make management choose demolition over restoration. Too bad, too, because just before the crash, rumors flew through the college radio station that the Stones would book the hall for old time's sake on their latest mega-tour.

The Dead played Swing Auditorium a handful of times, including the classic show in February 1977 when they opened with the debut of "Terrapin Station."

Swing Auditorium wasn't crowded on January 6, 1978. An audience of a few thousand

and festival seating made this the only Dead concert where I was able to get fairly close to the stage. So I'm standing less than fifty feet away, excited about what was to come, when they launch into Jerry's first song — and his voice is shot! He sounds like a sick frog, croaking out the words. A cold hammered his throat bad.

When his next song came he belted it out as best he could, his voice strained and groaning with every phrase. It was painful just listening to the vocal carnage, but Jerry wanted to sing! He was trying to force his way past the problem. And on his next song, he continued to bull his way through, desperately trying to get the words out as his voice degenerated into a coarse, raspy whisper, eventually cracking and breaking up completely. Finally he admitted defeat, stopped singing entirely, and concentrated on his guitar playing the rest of the night. But damn it, he tried. He tried with all his heart to get to that special

place he wanted to be, playing the music and singing his songs to us. He tried, even though he was sick, even though the crowd wasn't huge, even though the building was drab. Jerry wanted to share himself with us. He wanted to share his vision of joy and beauty, whatever it took. Jerry had heart, and I miss him.

A L A N   B U D R I S

I remember at the '83 Greeks when Bobby was really getting off on the HAHHHs near the end of "Estimated Prophet." As another one came around again, at the exact same time that Bobby HAHHHed to the crowd, Jerry mouthed the same with a big grin on his face, looked around to see if anyone in the band saw him, then went back down to his guitar. Really cracked me up.

M O N T I   M O O R E

In 1965, I was all of fifteen, going to a very snooty girls' boarding school in Palo Alto. We were required to learn an instrument. The school preferred a classical instrument, but my mom marched me into Dana Morgan's guitar shop in Palo Alto and I picked out the most expensive electric guitar I could find, a beautiful Cherrywood Epiphone solid-body Guitar. Jerry was to be my teacher.

I was embarrassed because I felt dumb in my little uniform, plaid skirt, black-and-white loafers, a middy blouse with blazer and tie. My chaperone had to wait in the front while Jerry took me to the back, handed me the guitar, and asked me to play something so he could see where to start. Little did I know that the Cherrywood Epiphone guitar was his favorite instrument in the shop. This little teenybopper had picked it out.

I began with the only song I knew: "Pipeline," a sixties surf tune. My rendition was very bad. He could have laughed; he could have insulted me, a dumb kid who had picked out his favorite guitar and was butchering even "Pipeline." Instead, he began to play—incredible music of a kind that I had never been exposed to—real, heartfelt music.

My life changed. Something was happening here. I didn't know what it was, but my value system was beginning to be altered by a level of creativity and beauty that allowed me to begin to choose other options.

That was my last year at the boarding school. By the next year, I was going to Pacific High School, a Quaker-run alternative school in Woodside. I became deeply involved in the peace movements of the sixties, and I danced onstage with the Dead

at the first Acid Tests at Fisherman's Wharf.

Was it the guitar? No, I really never learned to play well. Was it Jerry and his music? Yes, I think it was. Why? Because I was a dumb little kid and he took the time to be kind, and to play for me, and to encourage the artist in me — in a real way, not a book or a grade, but . . . "You want to dance?" Jerry said. "Then dance. No rules, just dance."

DON PASEWARK

My first show was March 15, 1973, at Nassau Coliseum. This was the first show after Pigpen's death. I was looking forward to seeing the Dead for some time, and I remember having fun at the show, but I distinctly remember the space was really weird. At the time, mirrored balls were "in" and every time I looked at the ball, I was eye to eye with one of the facets, and every time it came around, it appeared as a window to an

alternate universe. Like reading Huxley a few years later, I got an inkling as to what may be out there from Garcia and company.

I turned eighteen that summer, graduated high school, and with six of my friends embarked upon an adventure to Watkins Glen race track to see The Band, The Grateful Dead, and The Allman Brothers. Besides my friends traveling with me, we had made arrangements to meet others at the show. I made a flag, painted on a bed sheet—a really Byzantine skull with a rose between its teeth. Find the flag and that's where we'll be. We flew it at our campsite, and on Friday night we brought it to the sound check.

As the band was tuning up, Phil said something like, "There's some really nice banners out there, but we really like that skull with the rose between its teeth. You can really look through those eyes." Before I knew it, our flag and entire company of travelers were being escorted backstage.

A little confusion ensued; now that we were back there nobody knew quite what to do with us. The music was starting. I was there to see these guys and I was damned if

I was going to hang out somewhere where I couldn't really see or hear them. So I slipped out the gate and wound up in front, on Jerry's side. There I stayed, totally digging the music and the vibe from everyone around me. It was just so positive and great.

Then, halfway through the set, I heard the licks to "Bird Song." YEAH! I love that song! GREAT! Eyes closed, listening to Jerry and the band just go off, I truly hooked in, probably for the first time, to what this was really all about. About halfway through "Bird Song," I looked up and I noticed a spotlight shining on my flag, way up on the scaffolding, flapping in the breeze.

A couple of nights later, we went to see the boys again at Roosevelt Stadium in Jersey City. To my surprise, there was my flag again, happily flying on a warm and beautiful summer night. It made me very happy.

As an artist and musician, the Grateful Dead—and Jerry Garcia in particular—have had an incredibly huge influence on my work, my life, and my art. It is something I always wanted to thank them for. It is something I will never forget.

LAURA LEMAY

Three years ago or so, I was one of those pale vampire dress-all-in-black people you see in the Haight a lot. A friend of mine who I knew from the net asked me to go to a Dead show.

At the time, going to a Dead show was about the furthest thing from my mind. I was about as far from Dead-ness as anyone could be, being the hostile, angry little angst-ridden poseur that I was.

My friend, for mysterious reasons, campaigned with our other mutual friends to get me to go to this show. "I'll go," said I, capitulating, "but only if I can wear black. I won't wear tie-dye. But I'll go."

I went, and I sat on the lawn at Shoreline, being sullen and angry, as was my wont. But after a song or two, and after watching the people around me really enjoying themselves, I began, horror of horrors, to actually have a not-so-bad time.

And as things progressed, the not-so-bad time began to slowly slide into an oh-all-right-this-is-kind-of-fun time. And then, finally, into a OK-I-don't-care-who-sees-me-I'm-really-enjoying-myself time.

I danced. I laughed. I made friends with a couple of people who were not dressed in black. And they didn't care that I was. It was nifty.

    I had a lot of fun. It was definitely an experience I don't regret, and one that I'm happy my friends dragged me into.

    I regret the passing of Mssr. Garcia, because he and his cohorts made me open my eyes a little beyond my dark little world. And I understand the pain that his fans are feeling, because even though it was not my scene, I experienced a small bit of it and understand how good it was. I hope in some way it can continue to be good.

THE WHO AND THE DEAD, OAKLAND COLISEUM, OCTOBER 10, 1976
RICHARD McCAFFREY

OAKLAND AUDITORIUM, DECEMBER 31, 1979
RICHARD McCAFFREY

JIM WYRICK

On October 22, 1989, a few months after my mother died, two young friends took me to my first dead show in twenty-one years, in Charlotte, North Carolina. I was overwhelmed. Although I'm a fair musician, I'd never heard such music. It was as if I had lived all my life in black and white and then seen color for the first time. The spirituality and love were almost too much.

After the show we went to the Waffle House, a small all-night eatery with a counter and booths designed to seat about thirty people. Two very sweet, elderly African-American ladies were trying their best to feed 150 hungry hippies. I overheard them debating whether they should call their boss to ask for help. Finally, one of them headed for the pay phone at the entrance, and as she left she shouted to her partner, "I don't know about you, but I've had enough of this! I'm gonna call Jerry!"

The place went bonkers — 150 fried Deadheads cheering, laughing, clapping, and rolling on the floor, convulsed with hilarity. The poor woman froze in her tracks, having no idea what she had said. When things calmed down a bit, a girl asked her, "Do you have Jerry's number?" The lady sheepishly pointed to a number written on her palm and said "Yes, honey, I've got it right here"

DICK WATERMAN

Some years ago I asked Elizabeth Cotten (who was almost ninety at the time) if she was getting royalties for her song "Shake Sugaree" that had been done by The Grateful Dead as "Sugaree." She said that she had not, so I wrote a letter asking for an accounting. I got back a hailstorm of mail from their publisher, Ice Nine Music (Vonnegut fans will appreciate this irony), with a chapter and verse scolding about all of the Public Domain versions of the song prior to Ms. Cotten's copyright.

The matter was doomed at that point, but I had a chance conversation with John Scher, their East Coast promoter. I told him the story and he asked, "Does Jerry know about this?" I told him that I was quite sure that it had never come to his personal attention.

He told Jerry and wheels immediately went into motion. The decision was that she would not collect on "Sugaree" but they would do "Oh, Babe, It Ain't No Lie" on their next album and she would be given an advance on the writer's royalties. They sent her about $700.00 — very big money back then — and she went out and bought herself the biggest refrigerator/freezer on the market. It was the talk of the town.

I saw her some time later and asked if people were curious to know where she got the money to buy such a magnificent appliance.

"Oh, yes indeed," she said. "I just tell everybody it come to me as a gift from some dead people in California!"

R.I.P. good man Jerry Garcia . . . .

M A R Y   N E V I U S

After the middle Greek show, Summer Solstice 1987, Jerry was approaching his limo from the underground entrance and chanced upon the three of us waiting for him.

GIANTS STADIUM, NEW JERSEY, JUNE 19, 1995
PHILIP ANDELMAN

We had a yellow balloon with a picture of his face and a "We are everywhere" sticker. Jerry took one look at the balloon, removed the sticker, and affixed the sticker to his forehead with a chuckle. Then he signed his autograph "LOVE TO ALL NEW ENGLANDERS" (he never used lower-case letters).

S U S A N   A N D R E A   W E I N E R

A Jerry moment I'll never forget happened at the Keystone Berkeley. We were there to see the Nighthawks (I think), and Jerry walks in the back door. "What are you doing here?" someone at the pool table asked. "I'm here to play, I have a gig tonight," said Jerry. Except he was supposed to be at the Stone in San Francisco. He stood still, considering this, smiled sheepishly, and walked out.

R E E D   K I R K   R A H L M A N N

Here's another "I'm not a Deadhead, but . . ."

About a year ago I was called into a post-production house to do some background voice work for a movie. Crowd stuff and chatter. When setting up the appointment, the sound editor casually asked, "You're not into the Dead, are you?" I said no, and didn't give it much thought, figuring he might be mixing me up with someone else.

The next day there are about a dozen of us in this tiny studio, watching clips from this movie and making the appropriate crowd noises, adding the odd comment here and there where needed. To make things interesting, I started wisecracking as various characters, which this large bearded guy, who was also doing this voice gig, thought was pretty funny. So he started in, too. The two of us tried to see how far we could push it without completely pissing off the director/producer. She wore a tight smile through the whole thing, trying to laugh, too, but obviously feeling a little tense.

It turns out this guy was Jerry Garcia. The woman was his wife, and with all respect, the movie was . . . well, um . . . good-intentioned, anyway. The reason I was asked if I was into the Dead (as I later found out everyone else had been asked as well) was because he didn't want any celebrity attention, but simply wanted to be a part of the crew.

Sadly, I never saw the Dead. Always thought I should, just to see what it was all about. I'll use this as a lesson not to take such opportunities for granted. Humans always seem to leave this planet faster than we expect.

In March 1993, I planned a vacation that would take me to Cleveland for the Richfield shows, then to DC for the Cap Centre, and up to Syracuse for the NCAA basketball tournament (like Bruce Hornsby, I am a hoops junkie). Well, that was the weekend of the superstorm that battered the east coast and canceled the Saturday Cleveland show. I managed to get to Cleveland through the storm and checked into the Ritz Carlton. That night, Jerry and Steve Parish came into the bar and sat down next to me. I didn't know Parish and said he looked like an old friend, Mike Stepanian, who I knew from my days with Pennsylvania NORML in the mid-1970s. Parish started to steam and Jerry said, "Uh-oh, wrong name to bring up, I'll have to apologize for my friend here."

We sat and talked for close to an hour before word filtered around the hotel and the place got nuts. He was aware of the case I was handling, said some nice things about NORML, and was funny and gracious. Signed everyone's scraps of paper and let them take photos. I will always remember him sitting there while a blizzard was raging outside and saying "Storm of the century, and I'm stuck in fucking Cleveland."

The other strong Jerry memory involves working out at the Four Seasons Hotel gym in Philadelphia with his wife Deborah. She was hitting the Stairmaster while Jerry walked the treadmill. One time, I was coming out of the pool and heading to the sauna (wasn't wearing my glasses), and I rounded the corner at the exact time Jerry was coming from the other direction heading toward the same (and only) sauna. I stopped, saw that he only had on a big towel and thought to myself, "There are two things in life I am not supposed to see. One is my parents doing it and the other is Garcia naked." I waved him on to the sauna, gave him a look that said I will respect your privacy (he had that Jerry smirk on), and went back to my hotel room.

ROBERT J. MCNAMARA

I was interviewing Jerry Garcia in the spring of 1982 in a hotel room in New York City and, for some reason, I thought to ask him what he'd been like as a child.

Garcia expressed some surprise at the question, but, as with most questions, he quickly got into it. "I was asthmatic," I recall him saying. "And because of that I had to go slower than the other kids. That's what got me into reading."

"You were a big reader as a kid?"

HAMPTON COLISEUM, VIRGINIA, MARCH 27, 1988
JOHN ROTTET

"Oh, yeah, that was it," he answered. He went on to say that he'd read constantly, yet school for him had been "some distant reality."

He smiled, and I recall him cracking that, "All that was perfect training for being a hippie." And then came a shrug and that great laugh.

Our conversation had turned to books. I mentioned that I'd been at a Dead show on Long Island the night before, and I'd seen Phil Lesh walking around backstage with a book in his hand.

Garcia told me that Phil had been reading a biography of Nicola Tesla. He added that it sounded like a great book, because Tesla was "a brilliant scientist, and just as weird as could be." I remember thinking it said something about Garcia that he cared to know what the people around him were reading.

US FESTIVAL, 1982
RICHARD McCAFFREY

I asked him what he had read lately that had impressed him. With no pause to think, he started telling me that Ken Kesey had recently given him a copy of a John Clellon Holmes novel, *The Horn*. Garcia became quite animated.

"It's really a musician's book," he said. "It's about a black bop musician, and it really does a great job of communicating a musician's head."

He urged me to pick up a copy of the book, and even mentioned that it was back in print in a new paperback edition.

We were going to get together for another interview session a week later, and, in the interim, I located a copy of the book and I started reading it. When I saw Garcia again I mentioned I was reading *The Horn*. He was obviously delighted. "Oh, man, that's great, you got it! Isn't that just the greatest book?" We talked about it briefly, and I always remember him saying that he thought the book had a "great texture" to it. That is, indeed, an apt way to describe the novel.

A few years later I interviewed him again. I mentioned that he'd given me good advice with *The Horn*, and I asked him what he'd read lately that he'd recommend. This time he mentioned *Lightning Bird,* by a writer named Lyall Watson. I'd never heard of it, and I asked him what it was like. "It's serious anthropology, but it reads like a novel," he said. "It's about a guy in Africa who walks into the bush with nothing but a bag of salt and a knife." That one took a while to locate, but I eventually found a copy of it, and, just like Garcia said, it was a great book. Over the years, I always looked for copies of *Lightning Bird* in used bookstores; I'd always buy any I found. I'd give them to friends, telling them, "Jerry Garcia told me to read this, and he recommends good books."

And that's a good way to remember him.

OAKLAND AUDITORIUM, DECEMBER 31, 1979
RICHARD McCAFFREY

CHIP CALLAHAN

The main thing I keep remembering about Jerry is that the last time I saw him was to share a blanket with him on the floor of the basement of the Grace Cathedral in San Francisco last Halloween, at a "Rave Mass" hosted by Matthew Fox. I was there just to check it out, being the curious guy that I am. It seemed that Jerry was there to do the same.

I was a little taken aback when he sat down next to me and I realized it was him, but he was pretty casual and very friendly, joking with me and my friend and the woman he came with. At one point the robed people leading the service stood at various places in the room, asking people to line up before them to be blessed with fire. They raised and lowered a small, hand-held flame in front of each person. Jerry poked me and told me to get the flame (we were still sitting down, and I was closer to the fire-bearer). I laughed and said something, then realized he was serious. He thought that each person should be able to bless themselves, or bless each other—he wanted to do away with the hierarchy of clergy.

When I didn't go after the flame he took it upon himself to go speak to the woman who had it, trying to tell her to pass it around and all. The woman obviously didn't know who he was and didn't understand what he was talking about (she, like all the folks running the service, was from England). She turned to me and asked what this "elderly gentleman" wanted from her. I tried to explain but she turned away. When I laughingly asked Jerry what he was getting us into he replied, emphatically, "I'm trying to get us into IT! IT!" and let out a good, serious laugh.

ALICE KAHN

I interviewed Jerry at his home in 1983-ish. Was to be my first real cash money journalism story. It took a long time to wake Jerry up and I thought I'd never get to meet him. He was sweet, sad, very smart, very humble, and kind of out-of-body. On the way home, I put the tape of the interview in the car, got so spaced out listening to it that I crashed into Dennis McNally's VW as he led me out into San Rafael. McNally, the Dead's publicist, was kind enough not to report the incident, but the money I made off the story went to restore his engine. A cosmic goof worthy of the Great Cosmic Goofster, RIP.

DRY
YOUR
EYES
ON
THE WIND

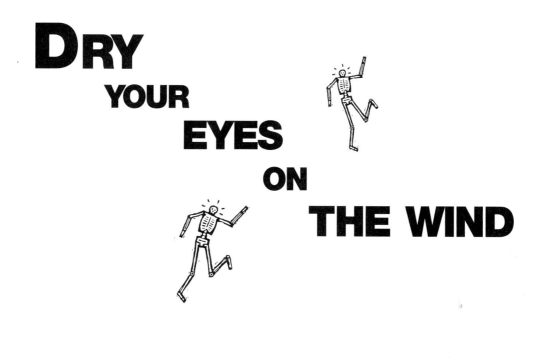

W A V Y   G R A V Y

"A Haiku for Jerry on the Day of His Demise"

The fat man rocks out

Hinges fall off heaven's door

"Come on in," sez Bill

WAVY GRAVY, HOGFARMER, SAN FRANCISCO, 1981
f-stop FITZGERALD

JOE GALLANT

Dear friend —

You will be loved and remembered for years to come. And justly so — few have been so blessed to serve as such a thorough conduit, entrusted to so regularly create the passageway.

To hear you was to hear a crystalline, cool-blue intelligence at play — sweet and dark, by turn; comforting and terrifying. And as the years added burnished weight to your phrases, the notes took on a gravity, a grace that spoke directly of your life, honestly of your struggles. In your hand, the commonplace became extraordinary, and the inspired glowed transcendent.

You've enhanced my life beyond measure, Jerry! Know, dear friend, your place deep in my heart.

HOWARD RHEINGOLD

There's a lot left of Jerry. And a lot of us in a lot of places are beginning to recognize it in ourselves, as never before. To have been around to have heard him while he was doing it live was pure grace, and I thank him for it now, as before.

BRIAN BOTHUN

Only today do I now fully understand how Elvis fans must have felt on August 16, 1977. Thanks, Jerry, for a real good time.

Reflecting today on the telephone with some of the bazillion people I've chatted with really makes me realize what a tremendous role Jerry played in my life — in all of our lives. It wasn't just the music, or the all-night car trips to or from some far-away venue, or any of the countless other things about being a Deadhead. It's about bringing people together and forging lifelong bonds with them. And Jerry, whether he liked it or not, was a driving force in so many lives.

I know my life was forever changed by Jerry Garcia and the Grateful Dead.

BOB BICKFORD

It's hard to get fully around the idea of Jerry Garcia dying. On the one hand, you

could say it's been expected and presaged for most of the last eight or ten years. Or more. On the other hand, it feels like the family patriarch, who's been there forever, has suddenly vanished; you can't quite internalize it. Not all at once.

We called a lot of our friends, including many people we hadn't talked to for a long time (we haven't worked at very many shows the last couple of years). Barbara, my wife's former mother-in-law, said she was glad she heard the news from us instead of impersonally, on the radio. There was a lot of that going around; the fans and crew of the Grateful Dead are the biggest extended family in the world, and many of us are very close indeed.

We also checked on what arrangements might be being made for some kind of service for crew and friends (we figured that the main service probably was private, or at least limited). Friday afternoon about 1 P.M. we got a call from a friend who has worked

with the Dead for many years, saying that he'd heard we'd be welcome at the service and telling us what time and where the van would pick us up, the name of the church, etc. We were startled, but deeply honored, and made ready to go (if you got an unexpected invitation to such an event, would you stay home?).

By 3:20 that afternoon we arrived at the pickup point and got on the van. When we got to the St. Stephen's church (appropriate!), it was surrounded by (naturally) police and (disgustingly) press. Upon checking with the staff, we found that there must have been some sort of misunderstanding, as the service was very definitely limited to family, band members, and only the closest of friends. Naturally, we left quickly, but we did have the chance to give a few special friends a hug or a handshake while waiting for a return shuttle.

Embarrassed, but still wanting to find something we could attend, we asked and were rewarded with the correct information: the event we wanted was at the Fillmore.

WINTERLAND, SAN FRANCISCO, OCTOBER 20. 1978
RICHARD McCAFFREY

Still private, but for staff, crew, and other close friends. We left immediately for it.

At the Fillmore, there were a lot of old friends in tie-dyes (we were rather overdressed, as it turned out!), some nice old Jerry Garcia songs playing, and a sort of "altar" on the stage with candles, a big picture of Jerry (the one with him appearing to do a magic trick, with a guitar neck rising out of a hat on the table in front of him), and lots of personal memorabilia. I wrote Wavy Gravy's beautiful haiku down and added that; someone else had the same idea, so there were two copies. Greta wrote a few lines of verse and left them there. There were numerous pictures, some professional and framed and some obviously amateur and loose. There were women spin-dancing, kids running in circles, and people hugging and talking, a few crying. It was painful, sad, cathartic, even joyful. It was a great way to begin the process of letting go.

We're trying to figure out what to do now. It's going to be hard to figure out how to stay in touch with the hundreds of coworkers, friends, and fans that we were so used to seeing at shows. It's going to be hard to figure out how to make do with only tapes of shows.

NEW RIDERS OF THE PURPLE SAGE, WINTERLAND, DECEMBER 31, 1977
RICHARD McCAFFREY

Greta asked me, "What are we going to do? How will we keep the magic that was the shows?" I could only say "I guess . . . we'll just have to live it."

DREW TROTT

There were a lot of red-rimmed eyes and, it seemed to me, a lot of short tempers. But I also saw a lot of peace signs and long hugs. And my, there was beauty. There were two flocks of doves; I didn't see them released, but I heard the crowd reacting to something. As we looked over we saw the two flocks wheeling overhead in formation, flashing white when they turned broadside to the sun, almost disappearing when they turned edge-on. They see-sawed off to the northeast.

Then came the two biplanes, around 2:00. One towed a sign that said, "Jerry Loves You." That reduced about half the people around me to tears. (It was hard to count them through my own!) Then the other biplane started dropping armloads of carnations that plumed out behind the plane and drifted down into the crowd. I saw one guy going from person to person with a carnation, offering each a sniff — a fitting kind of communion.

RHAN WILSON

(with K. Salazar)

My View from the Stage

This is my story of one of the most memorable days in my life.

On Saturday night, the 12th of August, I was at the Icon in San Francisco setting up my gear for a gig with the band I'm in, Haunted By Waters. I had been thinking a lot about Jerry Garcia ever since the news of his death hit me the Wednesday before. Tonight, I decided, I would play the best that I could, in his honor, and not be as self-conscious as I usually am, and just be happy and thankful.

When my bandmate Bean showed up, I told her I was thinking of Jerry and had spoken his name more in the last few days than in several years previous. She asked, with a smile, if I wanted to say it one more time. "I just got a call from my friend Chalo Eduardo, and he said that Mickey Hart wants to get a bunch of drummers together to form a procession at the memorial tomorrow. Chalo asked me to join him but I can't, so I gave him your name. He wants you to bring a snare drum. Zakir will be there, and—"

"Are you kidding?" I exclaimed, somewhat astonished. She assured me she was not. "But I don't have a snare drum!"

"You can use the one from our drum set," said Bean. She handed me a post-it note which read: Meet at BGP [Bill Graham Presents] on 5th between Howard & Folsom @ 8:00-8:15. Bus leaves @ 8:30.

That evening I played better than I had in a long time. My feelings of excitement were mixed with sadness at what I was about to be a part of. I would be in the company of many of my musical heroes, yet this was a time to pay respect to Jerry, not to be star-struck.

I didn't sleep much that night, but I woke up promptly at 6 A.M. I needed time to make a strap for the snare drum. I don't remember if I ate, although I must have had coffee. All I could think about was that I had to get there by 8 and I had to have all my shit together.

My housemate gave me a ride to BGP. As he was dropping me off, he pointed and said, "There's Mickey!" I approached Mickey, introduced myself, shook his hand and explained I was looking for Chalo. He told me he hadn't arrived yet and to just hang out. So there I was, with my backpack and snare drum, trying not to act as nervous as I felt. I noticed myself shivering a bit, due to a combination of nerves and the chilly morning air.

As others began arriving I asked each one if he was Chalo, as if finding him would somehow make my being there more official. Baba Olatunji was one of the first to arrive. Then Zakir Hussain and his daughter. Armando Peraza was in the parking lot talking

GIANTS STADIUM, NEW JERSEY, JUNE 19, 1995
PHILIP ANDELMAN

when I heard someone mention the name Michael. I looked in that direction and there was Michael Shrieve walking around. Everyone was shaking hands and asking about each other's health and families.

My nervousness was slowly being ousted by a sense of friendship and caring. These weren't stars here this morning, these were friends gathering to pay respect to a friend and fellow musician. I walked up to Zakir, one of my newest heroes, and introduced myself. "Hi, I'm Zakir," he responded in a friendly manner. As if I didn't already know that.

I recognized Shale Love, who I had seen before at drum circles. We were talking about what we were about to become a part of when a van pulled up and someone called out, "Finally, there's Chalo." I walked up to him but before I could say anything Chalo looked at me with a sense of instant recognition and said, "Hello. Rhan, right?"

The buses were now ready. We packed the drums in the storage compartment and took our seats. Why weren't we moving? Well, Mickey had decided it would be nice for us all to have coffee, so he sent someone to buy some. When the coffee arrived we de-bused, got our cups of java and got back on the bus again.

Everyone was talking on the way over. Armando was speaking Spanish to Jorje Bermudez, and Shale and I were talking to this guy across the aisle who lives in L.A. He told us he was having dinner the night before when he got a call from Chalo asking him to participate. He drove all the way up here through the night, drinking iced cappuccino, trying not to nod off while driving.

This was a historic happening and we all knew it.

The bus driver was a no-nonsense kinda guy who had earlier directed us all to put our drums in the back and get moving. He didn't say much on the way to the Polo Field, but when we got to the entrance, which was blocked off and guarded by security, that all changed. The security guys told us no buses were allowed to pass.

With a serious tone the driver informed them: "We're with BGP."

Looking a little confused, the security guy responded, "We're not supposed to let any vehicles in."

"We're with the Grateful Dead!" the driver said with authority.

As the guards repeated, "They're with the Grateful Dead," they pulled back the barriers and let us through. We all laughed. It reminded me of the scene in *Star Wars* when Obi-Wan Kenobi tells the guards, "These are not the droids you are looking for. We are OK to pass." Hypnotized by the "force," the guards repeated Obi-Wan's words and let them pass.

GOLDEN GATE PARK. CIRCA 1975
RICHARD McCAFFREY

We got off the bus near the tunnel that leads to the Polo Field. Mickey strapped on a "surdo" (a BIG bass drum used for the samba), and gathered us all around. He demonstrated a simple rhythm and asked us all to play it slowly. "Don't rush," he said. "Relax."

I saw that we had been joined by Phil Lesh, Bill Kreutzmann, and Bob Weir. Bill had a big talking drum he planned on playing, but when he went to hit it, the whole head ripped off. "It was an old drum," he said. He asked Shale, "do you have anything else in your bag? Some claves or something?" A car drove up and out stepped Vince Welnick.

A man in a wheelchair called out and told Phil how much the Dead made him happy. Phil spoke with him for a long time, smiling and shaking his hand. I could see the guy was again filled with the love the Dead can bring.

I was standing next to Zakir. He was playing a little hand drum, one that he used to open his shows. I asked him how in the world he can play so damn fast. "I know this isn't the time for a lesson, but how should I be using my fingers to get those rolls that you do?"

"The triplets are the easiest, " he answered, and showed me how to do them. "See, you need total control and strength in each finger."

By this time I was surrounded by more famous and accomplished people than I thought I would ever meet in a lifetime, let alone in an hour and a half. We began practicing; Mickey emphasized the use of dynamics. He told us we would s-l-o-w-l-y be playing a samba-like rhythm through the tunnel, past the crowd and up to the stage. Baba would do some chanting while we played quietly, and then on cue we would stop. It would be time to address those gathered and talk about Jerry.

While I couldn't see all the crowd as I looked through the tunnel, I realized I would be playing in front of more people than I ever had before. But somehow I wasn't nervous anymore. We were all there for Jerry.

Security held back the crowd as we began playing, making our way through the tunnel and into the sunlight. I saw the outstretched arms, I heard the cries of "We love you," and I saw the looks of joy and sadness reflected on each face. I felt a sense of pride and honor I never before could have imagined.

The procession reached the stage. Just as I was about to step up a guard said, "The stage is too full. The rest of you wait here until it's over, and then you can lead the procession out."

What? Come this far to be left out at the last minute?! "Please," we asked, "let us go up there. There are only three of us left!"

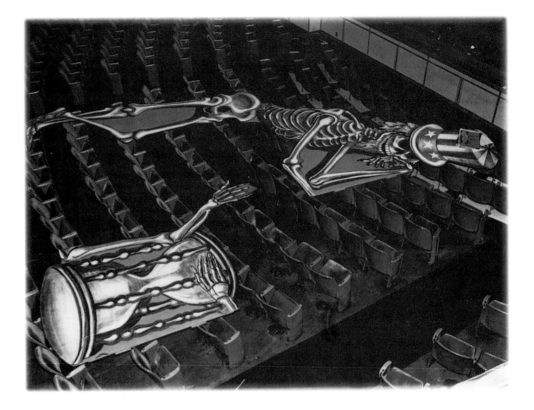

"Well, go on then," he said, somewhat reluctantly, and we quickly took our places as if he might change his mind.

I stood there looking out at everyone. They were my friends. Faces I'd never seen, names I didn't know, but friends nonetheless. They were holding pictures of Jerry, my friends, clapping and crying.

I was numb. I listened as Mickey told the crowd it was now up to them to carry on the love and energy the Dead had been giving all these years. One by one band members and associates spoke about what Jerry meant to them. I thought about what I was going to do and I realized that perhaps this wasn't just about Jerry, but about all of us —all of us caring, loving, giving, and most important, being in the now and appreciating the moment. This was how we best remember Jerry.

Mickey signaled us and we began the familiar beat we were to play next. He had told us earlier (mostly for those not familiar with the end-of-the-show tradition) that everyone would start singing "You know our love will not fade away." And of course that's exactly what happened. I thought for sure that I would start crying, but instead I just kept playing steadily and slowly, trying not to rush the beat.

I was trying to make eye contact with as many people as possible. Feeling a little more confident, I looked to Mickey for some nonverbal praise of sorts. He looked at me and said, "Relax."

Backstage, we stopped playing and dispersed. I got my backpack out of the bus and went over to check out the white tents that had been set up for the occasion. There was a wonderful catered lunch inside with all sorts of salads and pasta and, of course, Ben and Jerry's Cherry Garcia ice cream. I had a Coke and hungrily chowed down on what was probably my first meal of the day.

I mingled and thanked each and every person I could. I found Chalo and thanked him for inviting me. I saw Michael Shrieve, thanked him and told him how much he helped shape my adolescence. He seemed a little embarrassed by my declaration, but he thanked me.

I took time out to thank the higher powers that be for providing me an opportunity to be with all these great people and for the pleasure of having Jerry's music for all these years. I peeked out at the crowd from behind the stage and I felt comfort in knowing this couldn't be the end. All this caring, all this joy — I knew all this love simply would not ever fade away.

THE WHO AND THE DEAD PLAY OAKLAND COLISEUM, OCTOBER 10, 1976
RICHARD McCAFFREY

OAKLAND AUDITORIUM, JANUARY 1, 1980
RICHARD McCAFFREY

Thank you all, wherever you are, whoever you are. I love you all.

EMILY HOYER

It was sooo nice to congregate with the Dead family and have a 100% positive experience—strangers hugging tearful strangers, people cleaning up their trash, no vending presence (that I saw, anyway), great music (had a blast dancing to that "Scarlet-Fire," and was moved by the more somber selections as well).

On my way out, I was trying to pick up some trash before we threw ours out, and in the sizable section of lawn between our blanket and the receptacles, I couldn't find any—not even cigarette butts! Your garbage may vary, but I was impressed by the cleanliness of the place.

GORDON TAYLOR

I just got home from the most heart-wrenching yet uplifting tribute to Jerry Garcia.

I awoke at 5:15 A.M. to a clear morning sky, the almost full moon in its final descent. It was clear that Jerry wanted us to have a great time today. He succeeded by not letting one single cloud overhead, a steady cool breeze off the ocean nearby and some of the most intense good vibes I have ever felt in my entire life.

The actual set-up process began at midnight last night. About twenty or so BGP stagehands and others met at the Polo Field to build the scaffolding and stage. Some of us who volunteered our time to this had just come from the KMEL Summer Jam '95 at Shoreline, where thousands of fans of a very popular gangsta rap group—whose name escapes me —rioted because their concert was cut short due to numerous gang fights and other incidents in and around the amphitheater (including one in a backstage dressing room). The demanding task of switching emotions was difficult and ironic. One event shows human decency gone out of control with no regard to human value and life, and the other event is the polar opposite.

Musical Selection by Dick Latvala and our very own David Gans! Sound by Ultra Sound.

At 10 A.M. the procession began, led by a Chinese dragon, which was followed by a legion of drummers led by Mickey Hart and the rest of the Grateful Dead. Beginning from the right of the stage, it circled the upper perimeter until it reached the other side. Once there, they were joined onstage by many staff members as well as Paul Kantner and Wavy Gravy. Each had something to say, and all of it was perfect. It

was Bob who seemed the most devastated: he had a difficult time getting through to the end of his message.

At about 2:30 an airplane circled overhead, towing a banner that read "Jerry Loves You!" A second plane crisscrossed the length of the field at a lower altitude. It made two passes, and on the third pass it dropped hundreds of red and white carnations.

The Final Song was, appropriately, "I Bid You Good Night," which sent a lot of us to tears. As the the song ended, all those left backstage knew this was it. This was the moment where it was laid down for one last time.

Jerry was still flying high on that scaffolding frame for us and the milling crowd while we tried to pay attention to getting on with our lives. On either side of Jerry's portrait were

four of the triangular screens that GD had used as part of the stage set. When it came time to strike all the hanging stuff, including Jerry, not one person said a word and we avoided taking Jerry down until all the other pieces had been taken down.

And then it was time for "Jerry's Final Load Out." We tied two ropes to the top of the portrait, one on each side, and proceeded to loosen the brackets that held it in place. One of the brackets refused to come loose, and while we were struggling with it the people remaining on the field noticed that Jerry was about to come down. At one end of the field someone began to blow a conch shell, and a slow, steady roar began to build. Just as the conch shell silenced, that bracket came undone and we began to lower Jerry and roll up the portrait, having been instructed to be very careful of wrinkles. We then carried it over to the truck and he was gone. Once again I was reduced to tears.

I'd thought you'd all like to know—especially those who were able to place something on the shrine in the Polo Field: All of those items, flowers included, were gathered up very, very carefully and placed in boxes. The flowers were tied in bunches and then tied to long poles so they could be hung for drying (or so it appeared). If you have wondered what would happen to whatever it was that you gave to Jerry's shrines, you can be sure that it was carefully preserved. The portrait that hung above the stage went to Ram Rod's house.

RITA HURAULT

I was very lucky to find myself in a place of honor and service: I carried offerings for the altar and placed them with love for the people who weren't allowed on the other side of the fence.

There were (the short list): flowers, beads, crystals, pot, rings, shoes, socks, hats, tee shirts, photos, cookies, candles, incense, balloons, buds, earrings, poems, prose, sobriety coins, pinwheels, prayer flags, drawings, rocks, guitar picks, zucchini (3!), troll dolls, a tiny Barbie, bread, rose petals, Buddhas, devas, saints, Madonnas, wrapped-up satchels.

I think any day that you can see a zucchini as a sacred object is a special day.

It was one of the most amazing and profound days of my life and I feel very blessed.

KATHY WATKINS

The Polo Fields was like one last show. We spread out our blankets, hugged old friends, napped in the sunshine, and danced to beautiful music. The sadness came in waves, interspersed with gratitude and wonder that we had experienced so many unspeakably beautiful moments with this band and with each other.

Almost every person I spoke to talked of the need to go out and create something positive now. To continue the story of a group of people, determined to celebrate life and living. Stubbornly seeking beauty. Frankly wallowing in their love for each other.

Something new is waiting to be born.

JOE OLIVENBAUM

Went to the gathering last night in Central Park. Didn't help much. Some of it was like a parking lot scene — like we can't get together without it being a party. Cause it's always been a party. As the evening went on, it became more folks just sitting quietly, burning candles, saying little. Just made me sadder — will we ever gather together again? Those paraphernalia — tie dyes and tour shirts, which I always thought were usually cheesy and just this side of bogus . . . not bogus anymore.

Took the train to get there. Waiting for the train, saw a woman I figured was going where I was going. Just walked up to her, started talking . . . had an hour-long conversation with a complete stranger. Just the sort of thing that happens at shows. Ever again? Where else can you find a whole lot of people with so little fear of each other?

ALYSSA COTLER

I brought my grandmother along. She had never even heard of Jerry before last week, but knew I was a Deadhead. This eighty-year-old woman loved the scene. She said it was beautiful to see so many different kinds of people who were so friendly (being from Brooklyn, she doesn't get a lot of that). She thought it was "mean" that the cops wouldn't let some people have drum circles. Said she was disappointed that she can never go to a show.

Goes to show you the widespread appeal our community still holds. Thanks everyone for always making everyone feel welcome.

C A R O L Y N   G A R C I A

Well, I guess we started this out last week by getting that phone call . . . and I didn't believe it, 'cause we've gotten phone calls like that before about Jerry, that rumor had it he had died or was in a coma or . . . It really took a while to sink in, and I think it's taken until now for the family to begin to understand what's going on. And my heart goes out to everybody here, because we all feel as one at this time, and I hope that oneness can continue and go on. We've got each other. That's not so bad.

You know, and bless their hearts, they allowed all that taping. So that's the miracle of recorded music that we've got in our power. We set up a little altar at the house on Pigpen's old organ — I have one of the road organs — and we're putting the pictures up there and we found out later that some of the pictures weren't even of Jerry (laughs). But who could tell? And I went to my room to get the I Ching out, threw the I Ching and got "Before Completion" — 64th hexagram — which talks about the Book of Changes

as a book of the future. When we started, so long ago, we used the I Ching a lot. It kind
of fell out of fashion there for a while, but it sure rang true for me last week.

And then, as we were setting up the altar, I picked up my little runes. You know those
runes that come in a bag, they're really nice. And I got the second rune: Partnership. It's
an x, just a little x. "A gift. I am your beloved. You are my true companion. We meet in
the circle at the rainbow's center, coming together in wholeness, that is the gift of
freedom." And it's the rune that doesn't reverse, because the gift of freedom is that from
which flows all other gifts.

I know that Jerry lived in a passionate search for freedom for everybody, and it was
something so dear to him. We tried with the Rex Foundation to do some good in the war

on drugs, and the war on bad laws — we need to take that up. Truly, there's still a great need to pursue freedom.

I love you all and appreciate so much that y'all came down today to help me see how shared all this is, and may the sharing go on. Can we still have picnics and potlucks and stuff after this? And play music . . . Thank you.

August 14, 1995, at Alton Baker Park in Eugene, Oregon

MICHAEL BRANDT

Last weekend I climbed up to the top of Mt. Shasta, a 14,162-foot volcano in northern California. I carried with me white and red dried rose petals that I had collected and dried from the Jerry Memorial at the Fillmore and from my back yard. While climbing up, I met two other Deadheads from San Francisco's Richmond district. When we got to the top, we released the rose petals into the wind in remembrance of Jerry.

At the summit there is book to sign in. Looking through the book from the date of Jerry's death on, I noticed several people had previously made it to the summit and written poems and drawings in honor of Jerry. The Deadheads from the Richmond district pasted a GD backstage pass sticker on the inside cover of the metal box under the book.

I said some prayers then left the summit. It was an inspiring trip, and the closest I'll get to heaven for some time.

MIKAL GILMORE

In the summer of 1987, I wrote a feature-length cover story about the Grateful Dead for *Rolling Stone* magazine's Summer Issue. The experience of writing that article— which provided the magazine with one of its most popular issues of 1987—affected me as few other stories ever have. I was profoundly impressed by not only the band's music, but also the manner in which the Dead had kept faith with the same ideals that they began with.

My interest in the Grateful Dead and its music did not originate with undertaking the *Rolling Stone* assignment. Probably the first glimmer along these lines came when I saw the Dead perform a few years back on one of Willie Nelson's Farm Aid benefits. I had not seen the band live for some time — about ten years. In the late nineteen-sixties and early seventies, when I was living in Portland, Oregon, the Dead had been among my

favorite American bands; like countless other zealots, I saw the Dead whenever circum-
stance and money allowed. (I first caught the band during their Crystal Ballroom engagement
in which some of Anthem of the Sun was recorded, though perhaps my favorite show
from that period was a particularly exciting night at Springer's Ballroom.) But by the
nineteen-eighties I was a rock critic, and like a few other rock writers, I had grown to
assume that the Dead's best years were behind them. The last several shows I'd seen
by the group in the mid-seventiess (at Portland's Paramount) had seemed to meander a
bit for my taste, and by the time of the late seventies and early eighties, I was swept up
in the fervor of all the new revolutionary music coming out of the American and English
punk and postpunk scenes. (To this day, I don't apologize for that fervor: Like the San
Francisco explosion of the late sixties, the punk revolt was a great and fundamentally
transformative time.)

WINTERLAND CLOSED FOR GOOD, SAN FRANCISCO, JANUARY 1, 1979
RICHARD McCAFFREY

All this is to say that I wasn't really expecting that much from the Dead when the group appeared during Farm Aid on that July 4th, and yet what I saw impressed me more than anything I'd seen in a long, long time. It wasn't just that the band was good —damn good; in fact, as good as I'd ever seen them — but I was also struck that here was a band that clearly understood the meaning of playing together from the perspective of the long haul, with both a sense of history and a hard-won, deeply-held sense of fraternity. As a result, it was plain that the group understood not just the meaning of the words it sang, but also the meaning of the music itself, and what it meant to shape and push and discover, in a collective effort, that music's dimensions. Watching that afternoon, it seemed that the group members played as if they had spent their whole lives learning to play music as a way of talking to one another, and as if music were the language of their fellowship, and therefore their history. Nobody I'd seen in years had done anything remotely like that, and it struck me there and then, in that brief performance, that here was a band that had seen a long, hard, glorious and matchless road, and that they had learned to hold together and forge music as the bond of their affiliation. Here, I thought, was a great, too-little-reported story.

It was maybe a year later when I finally approached *Rolling Stone* to do a feature article about them. By this time, Jerry Garcia had gone through his court experience for the possession of hard drugs, and had also recovered from a near-fatal collapse into a diabetes-related coma. From what I'd heard, Garcia's regeneration had also amounted to something of a full-fledged renewal for the band: the Dead, reportedly, were performing some of the best shows in years, and were in the process of recording their first studio album in several years (In the Dark). I thought that writing about Garcia and the Dead's resurgence would help free me of my then-current obsession with the band (writing articles often helps me explore and fulfill my enthusiasm for a particular subject), but actually it only made it stronger.

Indeed, I came out of that experience not only newly impressed by the band, its musical prowess, intelligence, and sense of working community, but also impressed by the world of fans and fellow-believers that the group inspires. For many contemporary music fans — not merely the much-renowned baby boomers who came of age in the sixties, but also many younger eighties and nineties fans — the Dead provided a stirring alternative to the superficiality and mean-spiritedness that has preoccupied so much of pop in the last generation. As a result, the Dead was not simply another popular phenomenon that speaks for the moment—that is, not merely a band that found a

temporary place of fame and commodity in the ongoing chronicle of pop music. The Dead was something much bigger and more lasting, as well as something virtually unique in postwar musical history. For that matter, the Grateful Dead was a band that functioned as the binding central point to a large-scale alternative music scene: an audience that saw music as a crucial means of expressing a vision of a better, more hopeful and open-minded society.

I can't say I ever went on to be a Deadhead. Though I saw many of the band's shows in the late eighties, I saw few that I would honestly describe as transcendent. Still, there was kind of remarkable magic about what they did—making music into a lifetime fraternity that sustained not just the band's members and its organization economically, but that also nurtured a relentlessly large audience that found no better exemplar for its ideals and pleasures. Nobody else in pop music has done anything even remotely close. Jerry Garcia and the Grateful Dead took an ideal and made it into a more or less benign alternative nation, founded in a common faith in music and its ability to unify and uplift. I never saw them but what I admired them for their determination and longevity, and for what they gave, night after countless night, to their audiences.

There are those who will find it easy to dismiss all this—to claim that the Dead's endurance was simply a byproduct of a blithe nostalgia for a halcyon past that, truth be told, was never really neither too pacific nor innocent. There will also be those who claim that the Dead's experimentation with drugs—and its laissez-faire approach to imposing a code of moral behavior on both the band's members and their audience —in fact amounted to a rather pernicious influence, leading too many others into the wasteland of drug addiction. There may be some truth to these claims, but they don't amount to the most interesting truths. The Grateful Dead was one of the most popular, enduring, and significant groups in pop history, and perhaps the most misunderstood as well. They endured deaths and failures, blasted hopes and mainstream indifference, and despite all this, they created the largest and most continuous sense of hopeful community that rock and roll has ever produced. No doubt they enriched— and maybe even saved—a few lives in the process. Theirs was a wonderful and profoundly American adventure—a story of holding together through hard and dark times, and in the process, offering a model of faith and community to others who might need it. And that accomplishment is something that should not be dismissed too quickly or ridiculed too unthinkingly.

D A V I D   F R A N C I S

Thanks for the ride, Jerry

Thanks for teaching me to close my eyes to see . . .

Thanks for the excitment and anticipation of the next . . .

Thanks for showing me the courage to be who you are . . .

Thanks for being there, bent over, your glasses too low on your

nose and too engrossed in creation to push them up . . .

Thanks for offering your music to the world . . .

Thanks for bringing like-minded brothers and sisters together in

community,

For these are my dear ones today

Thanks for that grin you grin

Thanks for forgetting the words sometimes

Fare thee well, my Brother, I love you more than words can tell.

OAKLAND AUDITORIUM, DECEMBER 31, 1979
RICHARD McCAFFREY

I will always consider my year to consist of the three touring seasons: spring, summer, and fall.

I will always have a tough time getting up on those brutal, freezing mornings of February without the promise of spring tour to motivate my cold ass out of bed.

I will always have my friend Steven tune up my car in early March, although he doesn't know this yet.

I will always get my first haircut of the year at the end of April.

I will always visit the main post office in Manhattan one night in early May at 12:01 A.M.

I will always have more vacation days than I'll know what to do with in June. I will always use one of those days to change the oil in my car.

I will always wear my red white and blue tie-dye outfit, complete with socks and shoelaces, on the Fourth of July.

I will always celebrate Jerry's life and music, and the profound positive effects he had on my personality, psyche, and life, on his birthday, August 1.

I will always go to McSorley's Ale House on a Saturday afternoon in September and chug a waterfall of eight Lights.

I will always get my second haircut of the year at the end of October.

I will always have lower credit-card debt in November, but I will always resist the commercialism of the Christmas season.

I will always have unused sick days come the end of December.

I will always raise my glass and wish the bay area happy new year at 3 A.M. EST every January 1, and think back to another time in another space.

I will always remember how all of you here on the WELL helped me through one of the worst fuckin' times of my entire life.

I will always be a Deadhead.

WARFIELD THEATER, SAN FRANCISCO, 1980
RICHARD McCAFFREY

The following is a list of the music played at the Polo Field in Golden Gate Park on August 13, 1995.
Selections were programmed by Grateful Dead archivist Dick Latvala, assisted by David Gans.

Mississippi Halfstep- Wake of the Flood
Dark Star- 4/27/69
Sugaree-Garcia
Dark Star->Spanish jam- 2/11/70
Dire Wolf- Reckoning
Lovelight- 2/28/69
Days Between- Spring tour 1994 composite
St. Stephen- unknown 1968
Terrapin- 9/3/77
Doin' That Rag- 3/2/69
Mason's Children- 12/28/69
I've Been All Around This World- Bear's Choice
Good Lovin'- 4/10/71
jam (in Dark Star) - 9/19/70

Parade and ceremony

It's All Too Much->Iko Iko-3/18/95
Beautiful jam-> Dark Star- 2/18/71
Scary jam- 10/25/73
Alligator->Caution- 8/23/68
drums-> space-3/18/95
That's It for the Other One->New Potato Caboose->Born Cross-Eyed->
      Spanish jam- 2/14/68
Death Don't Have No Mercy- 9/29/89
Scarlet Begonias->Fire on the Mountain->Corrina->Matilda-3/23/95
Believe It or Not- 7/17/88
jam->bass solo- 2/24/73
Ramble On Rose- Europe '72
Sugar Magnolia- 9/7/73
jam- 9/21/72
Morning Dew- Europe '72
The Wheel -Garcia
St. Stephen -Live Dead
Box of Rain -American Beauty
I Bid You Good Night- unknown 1968

Greensleeves

Deborah Koons Garcia has asked that memorial contributions be made to:

Haight-Ashbury Free Medical Clinic
3330 Geary Blvd.
Second floor West
San Francisco, CA 94118

The authors would like to request that donations be offered to:

Rex Foundation
PO BOX 2204
San Anselmo, CA 94960

SEVA Foundation
8 North San Pedro Road
San Rafael, CA 94903